Instant! Interactive! Incredible!

Math Bulletin Boards That Teach

by Jacquelyn Johnson Howes

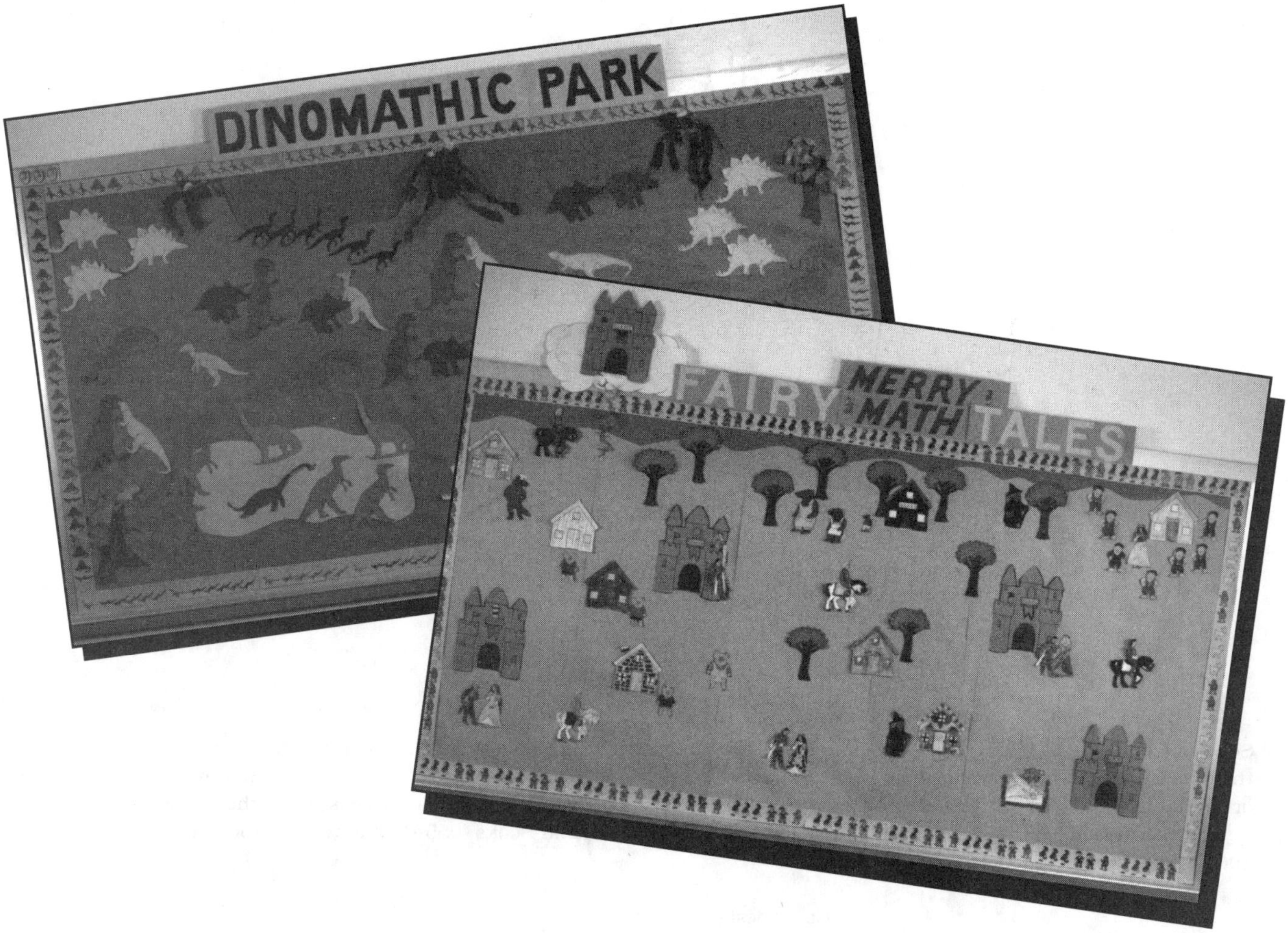

SCHOLASTIC
PROFESSIONAL BOOKS

New York • Toronto • London • Auckland • Sydney •
• Mexico City • New Delhi • Hong Kong

DEDICATION

To my children— Rick, Tommy, Steve, and Betsy— for always encouraging me. To my second grade class of 1997-98, who cut, colored, and did the math in this book. To my colleagues—Jean Evans, Kathy Geltzer, Donna Katsaounis, Nancy Shyer, and Joanne Simeone—who also did math murals and loved them, and to my principal, Henriette Camp and all of my colleagues at F.M. Kearns School. Also, to Nancy Snow and Wendy Anderson who painted large math murals on the hall walls at F.M. Kearns School in Granby, Connecticut.

Cover design by Norma Ortiz
Cover photographs by Donnelly Marks
Interior art for Oceans, Transportation, Insects, and Dinosaurs by Andrea Tachiera
Interior art for Fairy Tales by Delana Bettoli
Interior design by Grafica, Inc.
ISBN: 0-590-02905-3

TABLE OF CONTENTS

INTRODUCTION

What Is a Math Mural?

A math mural is a theme-based arrangement of specific numbers of characters or objects on a bulletin board, chalkboard, or white board. The purpose of a math mural is to give children hands-on, concrete experience in exploring basic math concepts. The themes provided in this book include: Oceans, Transportation, Insects, Fairy Tales, and Dinosaurs. For each of the themes, you'll find reproducible display items representing the amounts one through ten. For example, in the Fairy Tale unit, there are one wolf, two witches, three bears, and so on.

Why Use Math Murals?

Math murals are attractive, useful, versatile, and effective. They provide a real focus both for your classroom environment and for math lessons. According to an old Greek expression, "You learn from the things that happen to you." By having children cut out, color, and position the mural pieces, you involve children in the theme and generate pride in a class project. Because a math mural is interactive, children can see and do math using the items in the arrangement. You can use the mural again and again, either for practice or to explore new concepts.

What Math Concepts Can You Teach with Math Murals?

With a math mural, you can have children work on addition, subtraction, multiplication, division, estimation, counting, patterning, measuring, applying money concepts, and writing their own story problems. The borders provide opportunities for children to count by 2's, 5's, and 10's. You'll also find worksheets to use with each theme.

What Else Can You Teach with Math Murals?

Math murals are based on high-interest themes that easily fit into the rest of your curriculum. By using these themes for math, you are also broadening children's knowledge of subjects important in science, social studies, and literature.

Where and How Should You Display a Math Mural?

You can use any size bulletin board, chalkboard, or white board for a math mural. If you want the characters to be larger than the size provided in this book, simply enlarge them on a copy machine. For smaller characters, reduce the size. If you are sharing a math mural with another class, consider using a hall bulletin board and coordinating math schedules so that each group has sufficient time. Remember, also, to provide children with paper and clipboards if they are working in the hall.

If you use a magnetic chalkboard or white board for your math mural, you can draw the appropriate background on the board. Then glue a small magnet on the back of each character. By making the characters easily movable, you can set up problems such as these:

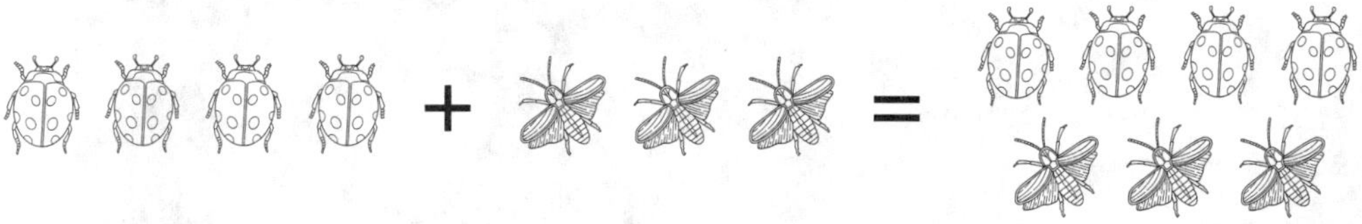

4 + 3 = 7

— or —

3 X 3 = 9

You can also use hook'n'loop fabric as the math mural background. This product, used with velcro, enables you to move characters around easily. It is 60 inches wide and comes in a variety of colors. To order, contact *Book Props, 16824 South Chapin Way, Lake Oswego, OR 97034,* and ask for word walls.

How Can You Adapt the Math Murals to Meet Students' Needs?

You can vary the number of items for a math mural display, or you can vary the amounts of each item. For example, instead of starting with 10 insects on a mural, you might begin with five. Or, you might decide to double the amounts of each insect so that there are two grasshoppers, four luna moths, and so on.

You can also use the mini-characters on page 90 and the blank concept sheets on pages 91-95 to create math sheets that meet the needs of your class. Be sure to have children create their own problems using these materials as well.

Oceans of Math

Talking About the Theme: Oceans

Children are fascinated by ocean life, and this interactive math bulletin board provides an opportunity to develop students' knowledge of the sea while practicing addition and subtraction skills. By creating this large and well-populated ocean on your classroom wall, you'll tap children's curiosity and bring math lessons to life.

After assembling this mural, I leave it up for four weeks and use it each day. However, the amount of time for using the Oceans bulletin board is flexible, and you'll want to adjust it to meet your own scheduling needs.

Materials

Before diving into this theme, you'll want to collect materials for assembling the bulletin board. You'll need:

- fish and sea creature patterns on pages 12-16
- border patterns on page 17
- roll of blue craft paper
- roll of brown craft (or wrapping) paper
- tan, light gray, dark gray, light blue, and white construction paper
- crayons or colored markers
- scissors
- stapler
- sand and glue (optional)

Getting Started with the Mini-Mural

On page 8, you'll find a reproducible mini-mural. This mini-mural serves two purposes: 1) it's a good way to introduce the theme and concept of mural math, and 2) it provides a template for the finished bulletin board display.

Make a copy of the mini-mural for each child. If necessary, identify each sea creature. You may wish to give students a chance to tell what they know about these animals. Then proceed with an informal lesson in which you tell stories about the animals. For example:

- The walruses are going to swim to the sea lions on the rock. When the walruses arrive, how many animals will be on the rock altogether?
- The manatees plus the killer whale equal 9 sea animals. What other combinations of sea animals will equal 9?

Continue in this way until children understand how to create math problems using the creatures on the mini-mural. Then explain that you are going to create a large bulletin board like the mini-mural.

Assembling the Math Mural

Follow these steps to create your Oceans math mural. You may wish to have children work in groups to prepare the different sea animals (steps 5 and 8) while you complete the ocean background.

1 Cover the bulletin board with blue craft paper to create an ocean background.

2 Cut out and staple strips of tan paper along the bottom of the board to make an ocean floor. Glue on sand for a more realistic effect.

3 Cut out three large brown rocks and staple them to the left side, right side, and middle of the board.

4 Duplicate the sea creature patterns on pages 12-16. You may choose to enlarge or reduce the images depending on the size of your bulletin board. I recommend the following amounts and colors, but you may wish to use others:

10 tan lobsters
9 tan octopuses
8 dark gray manatees
7 light gray dolphins
6 light gray porpoises
5 brown walruses
4 dark gray sharks
3 brown sea lions
2 white seals
1 white killer whale

5 Have children cut out the sea creatures. Ask a volunteer to color the top part of the killer whale black.

6 Staple the animals onto the ocean background. You can follow the arrangement on the mini-mural or invite students to help decide on another arrangement.

7 Duplicate the four border patterns on page 17 on light blue paper. Note that there is a different pattern for each side of the bulletin board.

8 Have children color the animals in the patterns as follows:

sea star = yellow
stingray = brown
crab = blue

9 Staple the borders along the bulletin board sides.

10 Duplicate the display title on page 11. Invite volunteers to color in the letters before you add them to the mural.

OCEANS OF MATH

Using the Oceans of Math Theme

You can use this math mural in many ways—for work in counting, addition, subtraction, multiplication, graphing, word problems, patterns, and estimation. You might begin by giving children problems such as these, then encourage them to make up their own problems. You'll also want to use the reproducible worksheets on pages 18-21.

Sample Story Problems

- The dolphins and porpoises are having a race. How many animals are competing altogether?
- How many fewer sea lions are there than sharks?
- There are 9 octopuses. How many octopus arms are there?

Sample Pattern Problem

- Should I add 2 or 3 starfish to continue this pattern? How do you know?

Sample Estimation

- How many crabs are in this pattern? How many crabs are in this top border?

Using the Worksheets

As children begin to make up their own math problems based on the bulletin board, provide them with these pages. You might wish to assign students to team up with partners to check one another's work.

Adding in the Sea

Explain to children that they should write number problems to match the pictures on the bulletin board. For example, for the first problem they would write 5 (walruses) and 3 (sea lions). Students should then complete the addition. Conclude by asking them how they can check their work.

Subtracting in the Sea

For this page, children again use the bulletin board to determine the number of animals for each problem.

Ocean Graphing

Students can use this page to make a graph showing how many of each kind of animal are in the bulletin board ocean. Once the graphs are completed, ask students to make up questions about them.

Model examples such as:

- How many lobsters are there?
- How many more manatees are there than sharks?
- Are there more sea lions or seals?

My Ocean Math Questions

On this page students create their own word problems. Explain that they can use any animal from the bulletin board. You might write the names of the animals on the chalkboard so children can spell them correctly. Or you can duplicate the mini-animals on page 90 for children to paste onto their pages. Note that item 6 involves measuring. Be sure to invite children to share their story problems with the class.

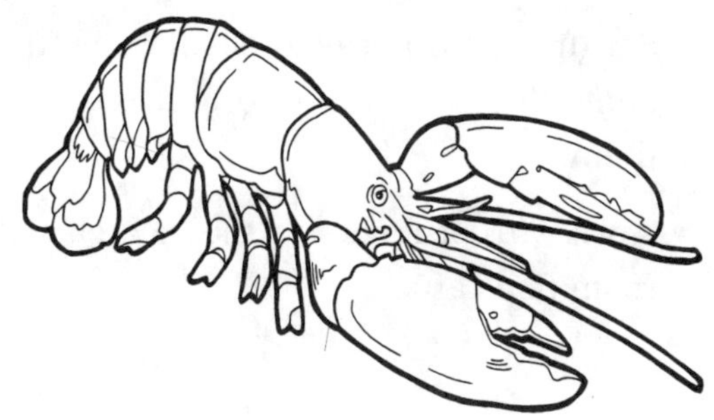

Cross-Curricular Activities

Language Arts

- Collect fiction and nonfiction books about oceans. Place these in a reading corner and encourage students to learn more about the animals on the bulletin board. Read aloud stories from a book such as *Nine True Dolphin Stories* by Margaret Davidson.
- Assign students to write a report about a sea mammal.
- Compile a list of new vocabulary words that come up as you use the Oceans bulletin board.

Science

- Teach a lesson on the differences between sea mammals and fish.
- Visit a local aquarium. Prepare questions to research beforehand.
- Set up an exhibit of shells. Have students find out who used to live in them.
- Work with students to set up a classroom fish tank.

Art

- Have students create paintings or collages of ocean life.
- Invite students to make 3-dimensional sea mammals and fish using clay, papier mâché, or salt-flour dough.

Social Studies

- Make a web to show how the ocean affects food, jobs, recreation, weather, and transportation.
- Study endangered sea creatures.

Literature Links

- *The Magic School Bus on the Ocean Floor* by Joanna Cole
- *Nine True Dolphin Stories* by Margaret Davidson
- *The Desert Beneath the Sea* by Ann McGovern
- *The Ocean Alphabet Book* by Jerry Pallotta
- *The Sea (The World Around Us* series) by Brian Williams

Oceans of Math: Reproducible Page

Use these letter patterns to name your math board. With the help of a Xerox copier you can enlarge each letter even more!

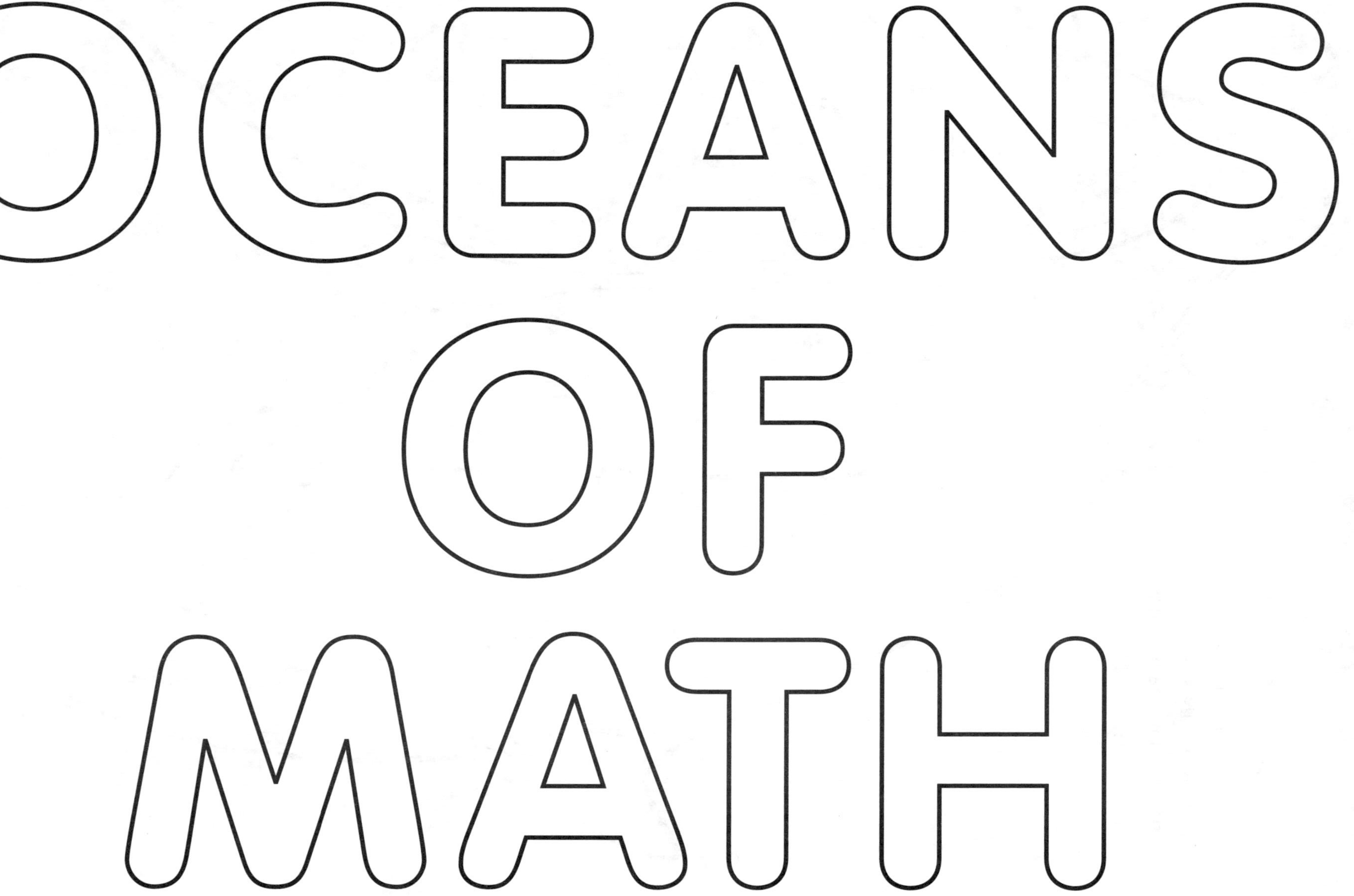

Oceans of Math: Reproducible Page

Copy on light gray paper. The numbers in parentheses suggest how many you will need of each pattern.

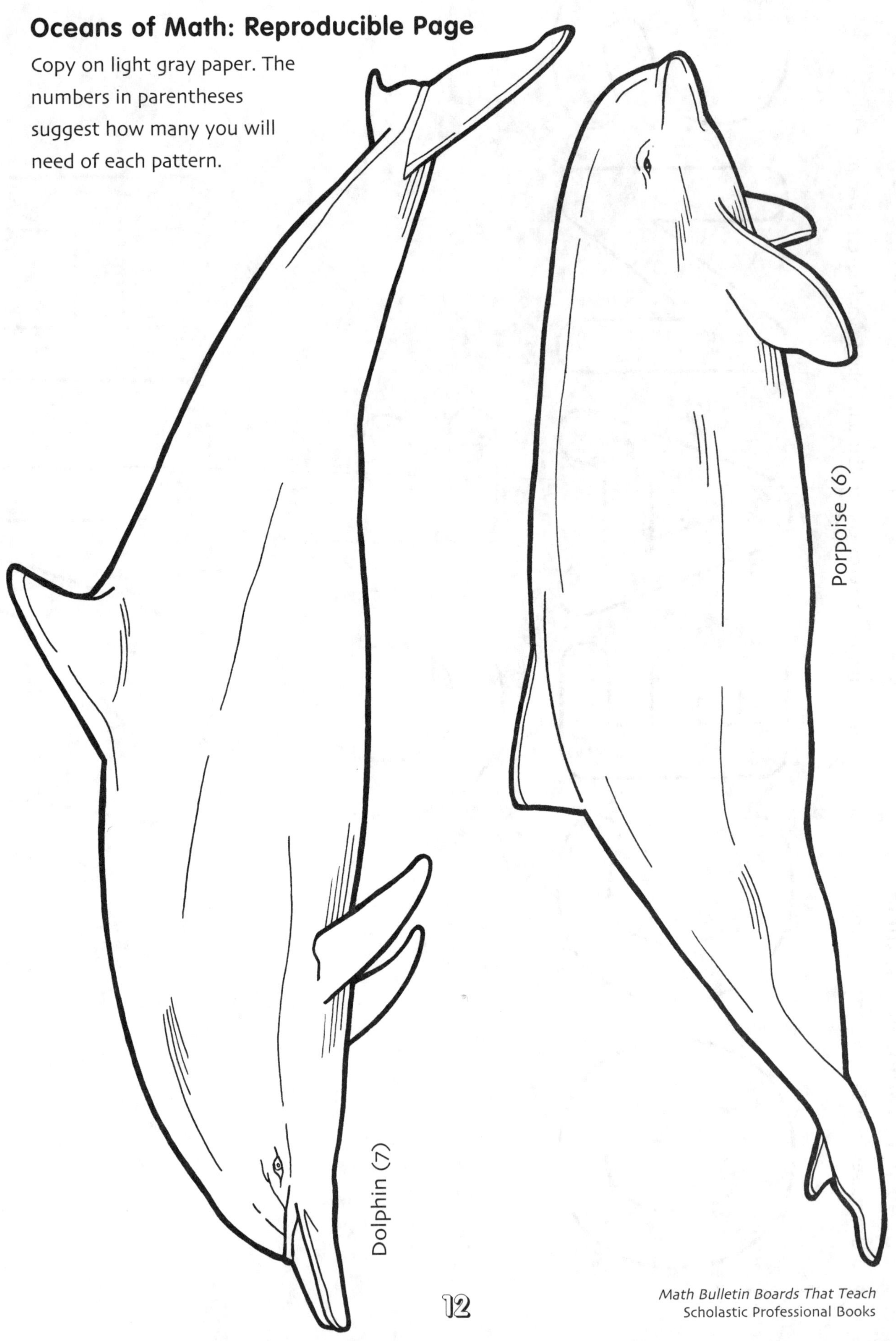

Oceans of Math: Reproducible Page

Copy on light tan paper. The numbers in parentheses suggest how many you will need of each pattern.

Octopus (9)

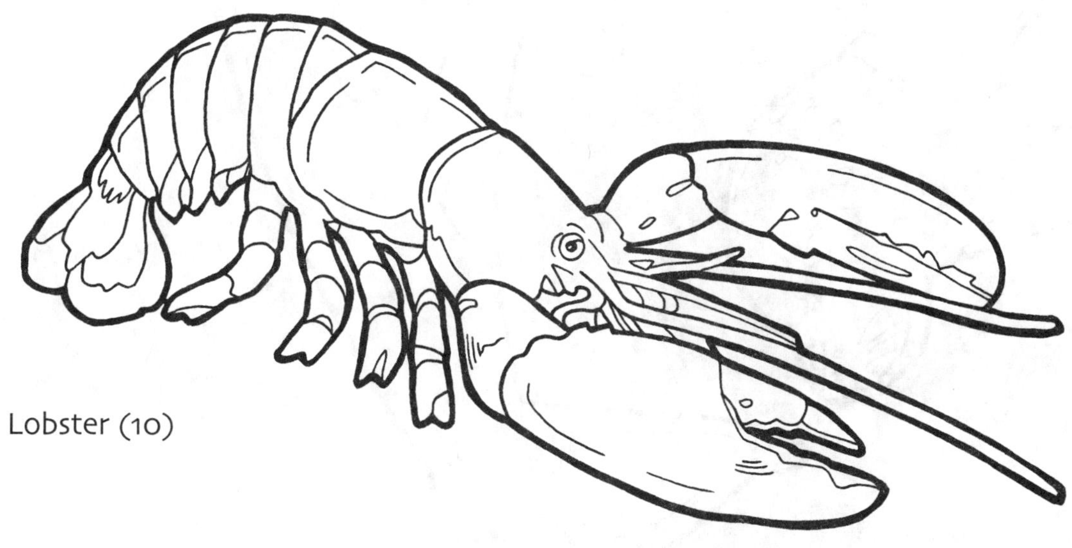

Lobster (10)

Oceans of Math: Reproducible Page

Copy on white paper. The numbers in parentheses suggest how many you will need of each pattern.

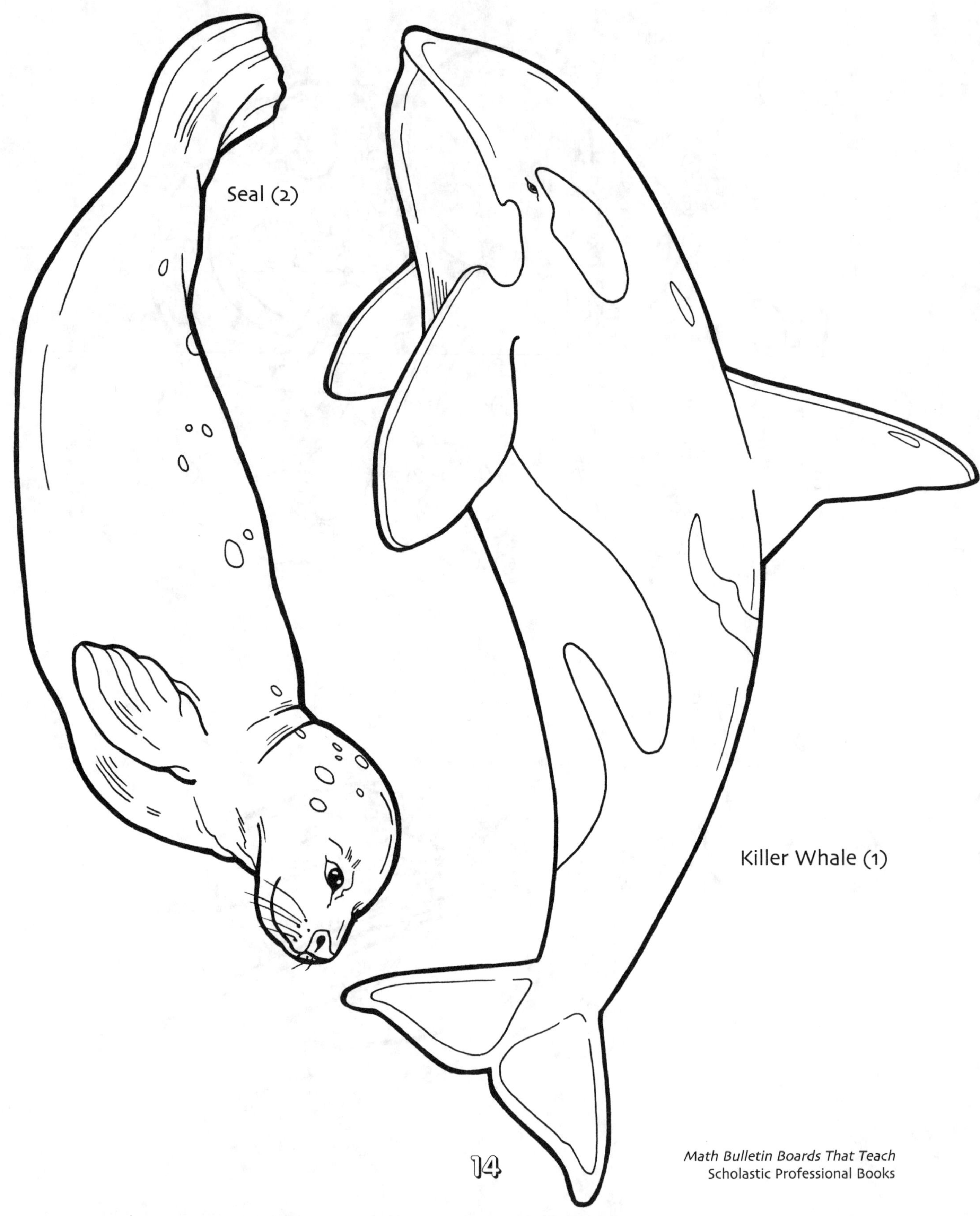

Oceans of Math: Reproducible Page

Copy on brown paper. The numbers in parentheses suggest how many you will need of each pattern.

Oceans of Math: Reproducible Page

Copy on dark gray paper. The numbers in parentheses suggest how many you will need of each pattern.

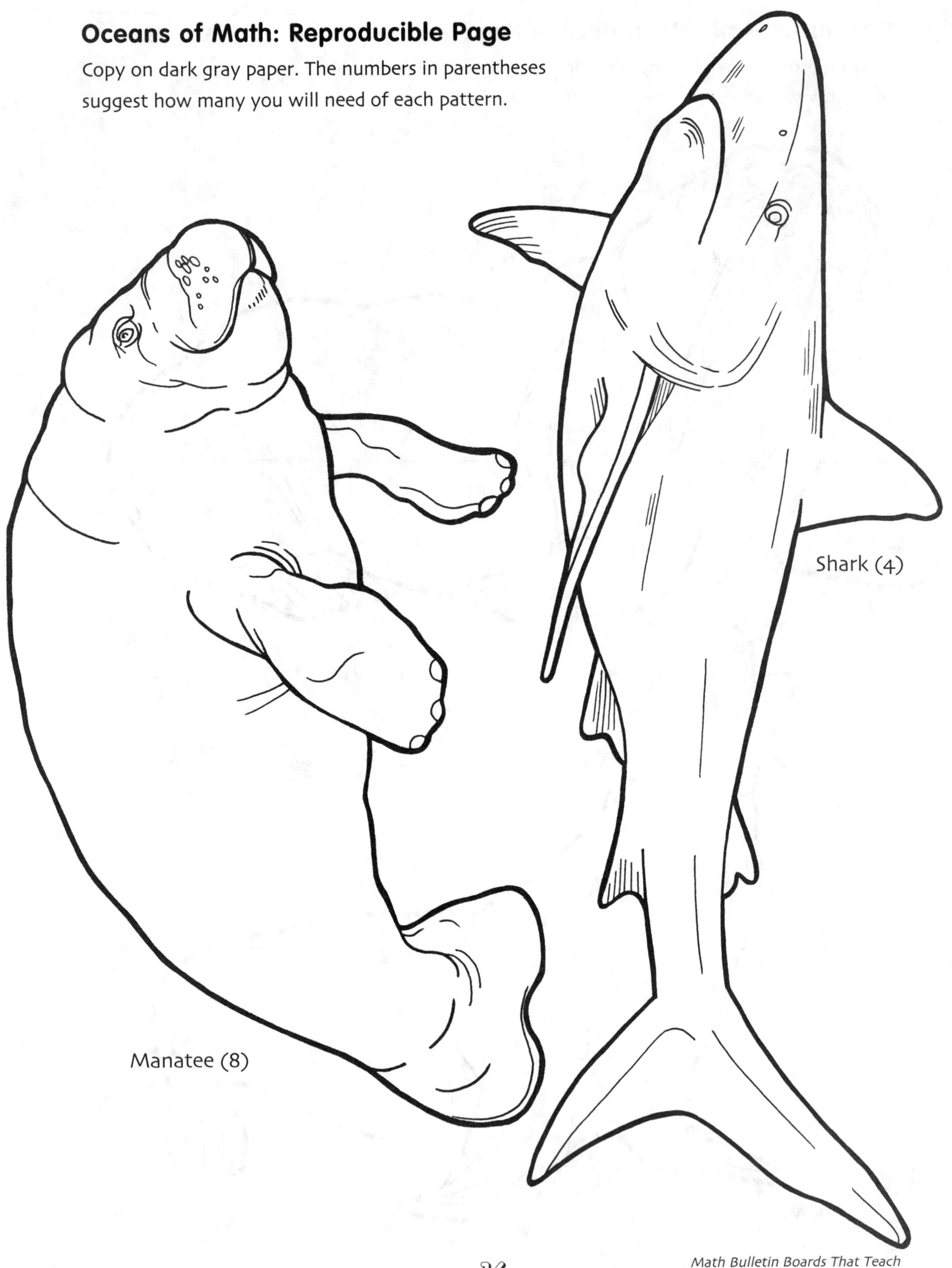

Oceans of Math: Reproducible Page Copy the border patterns on light blue paper. Have children color them as suggested on page 7.

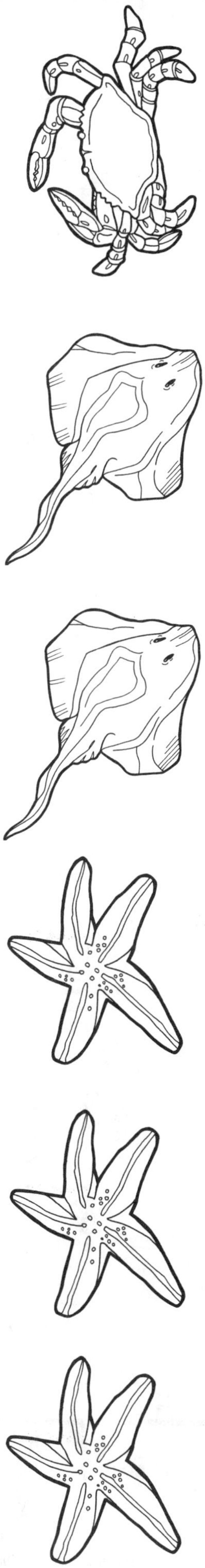

Top Border

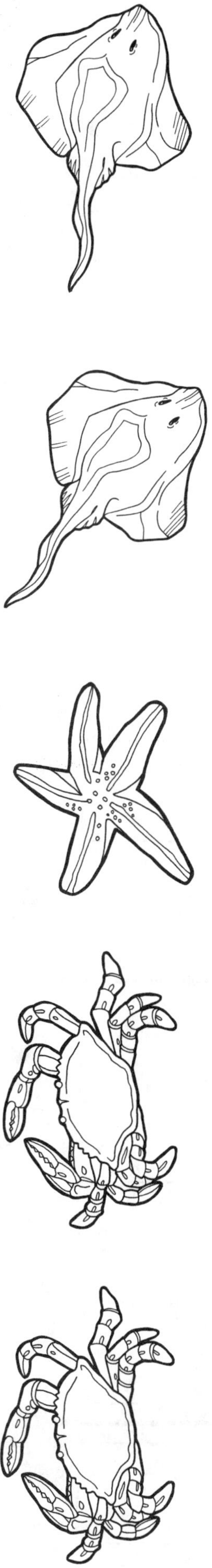

Bottom Border

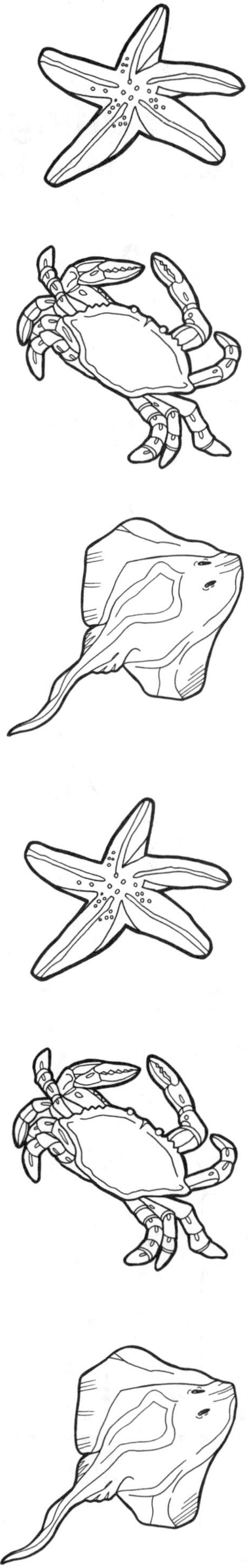

Right Border

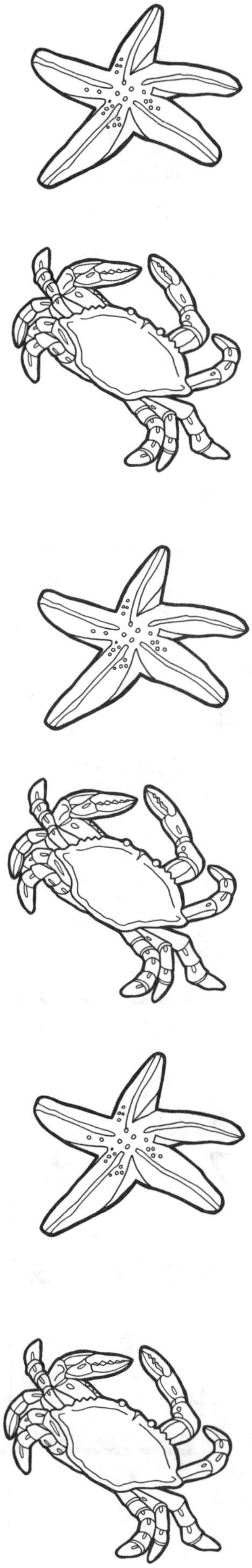

Left Border

Name: ______________________________

Adding in the Sea

Use the math mural to write the numbers in the squares.
Add the numbers.

1.

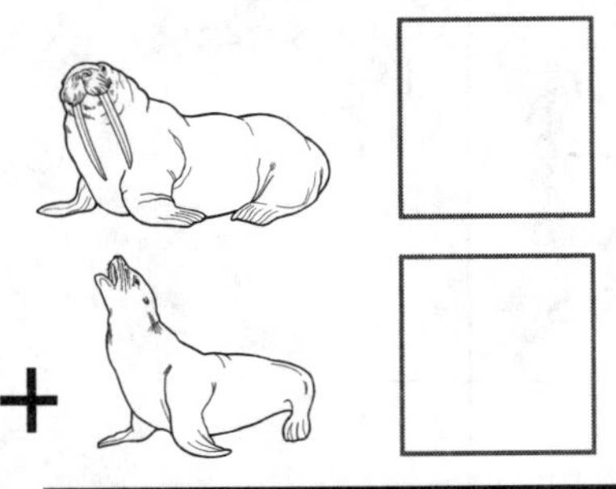

2.

3.

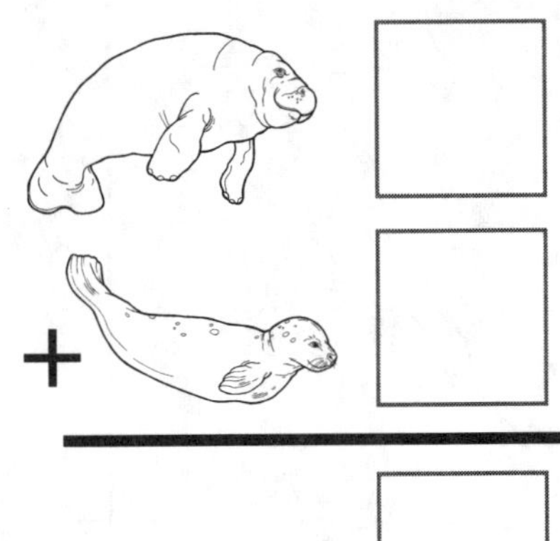

4.

5.

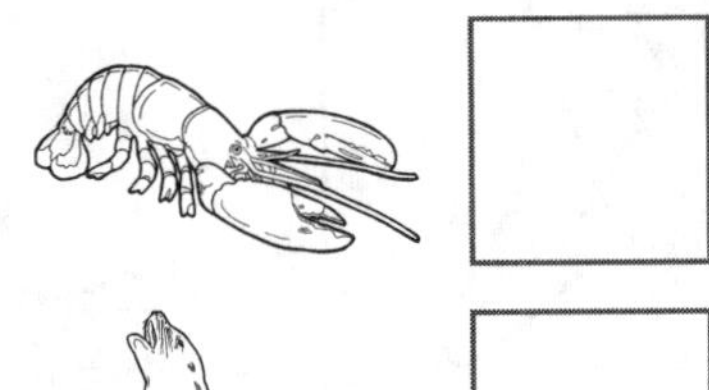

6.

7.

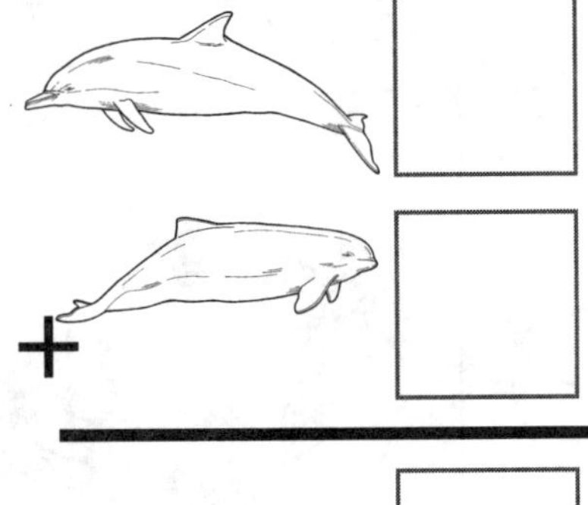

8.

9.

Name: ______________________________

Subtracting in the Sea

Use the math mural to write the numbers in the squares.
Subtract the numbers.

1.

−

2.

−

3.

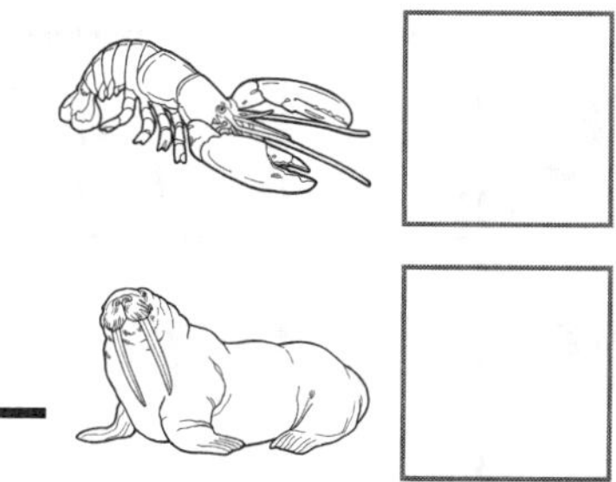

−

4.

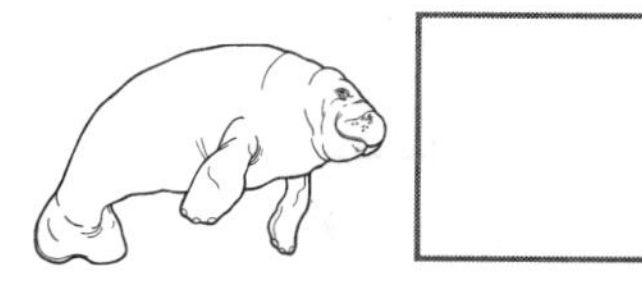

−

5.

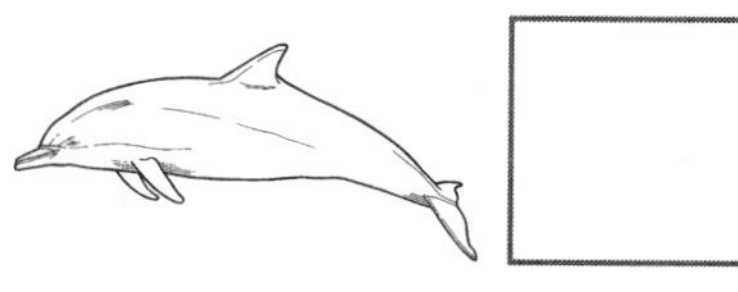

−

6.

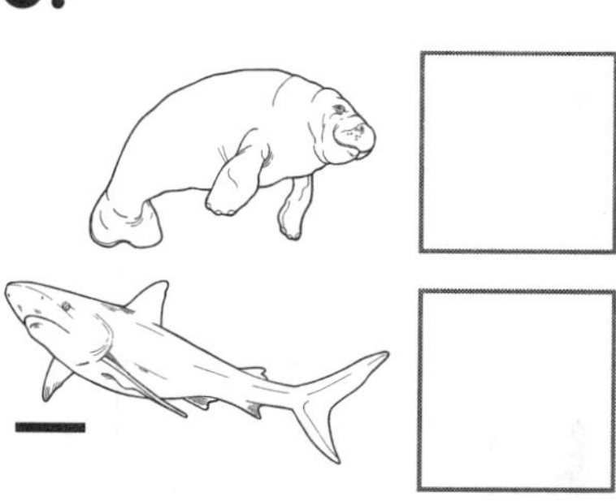

−

7.

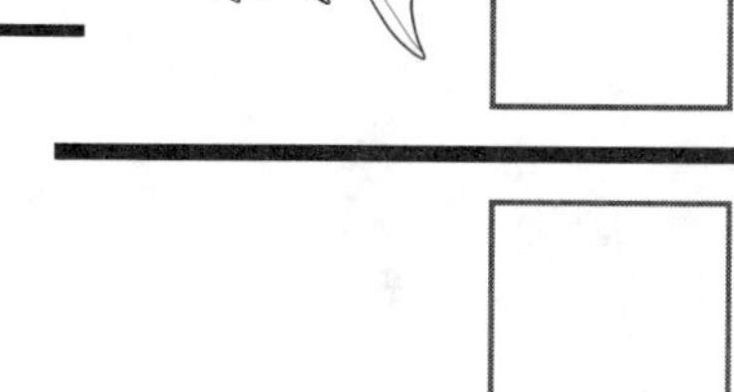

−

8.

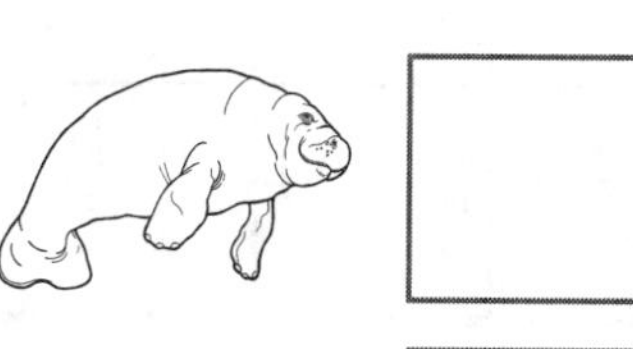

−

9.

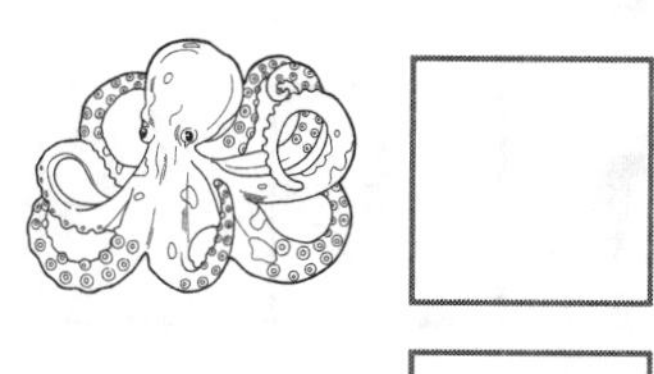

−

Name: ____________________

Ocean Graphing

Use the math mural to count the different sea animals.
Color the graph to show how many of each animal you count.

10
9
8
7
6
5
4
3
2
1

Name: ______________________________

My Ocean Math Questions

Make up your own math problems. Write the name of a sea animal on each line. Solve the problems.

1. How many ____________ and ____________ are there in all? ____________

2. How many more ____________ are there than ____________? ____________

3. Each ____________ eats two small fish a day. How many small fish will all the ____________ eat today? ____________

4. All of the ____________ eat five small fish a day. How many small fish will all of the ____________ eat today? ____________

5. How many ____________ and ____________ and ____________ are there in all? ____________

6. How much bigger is the ____________ than the ____________? ____________

7. Write a problem of your own.

____

____

____

Math-to-Go

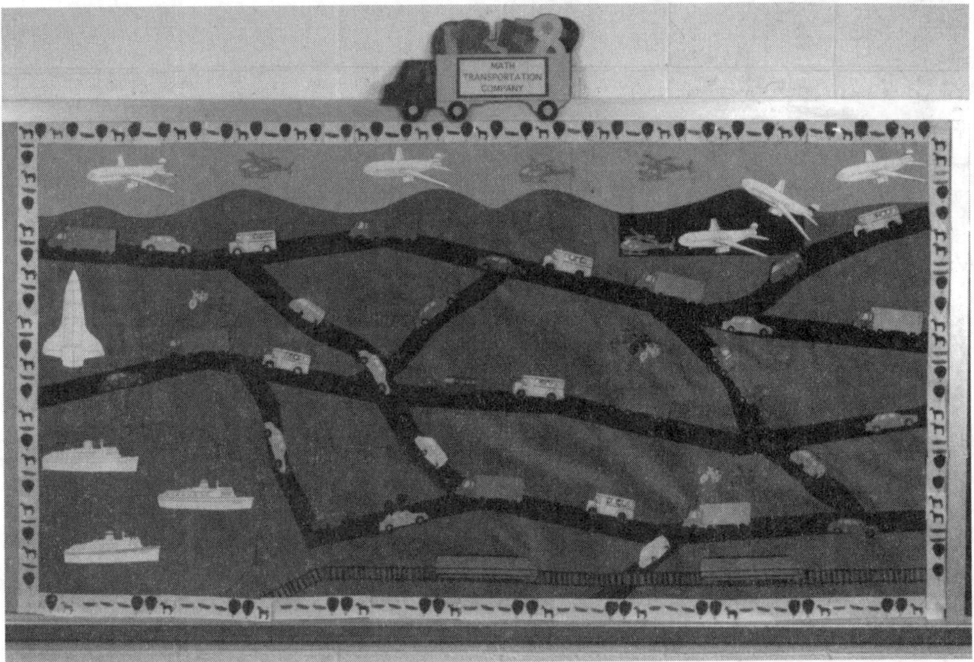

Talking About the Theme: Transportation

Most children like to go places and are already aware of some forms of travel. Many enjoy playing with toy cars and other small vehicles. This interactive transportation mural builds on children's interest while activating their math skills. As children work with the math mural, they will begin to internalize how math is all around them—everywhere they go.

Once you and the class create this bulletin board, you'll want to leave it up for several weeks. In addition to your math lessons, the mural will provide opportunities to explore many aspects of transportation.

Materials

The materials you need to assemble this math mural are:

- vehicle patterns on pages 28-32
- border patterns on page 33
- roll of green craft paper
- light blue, dark blue, black, yellow, gray, white, and brown construction paper
- crayons or colored markers
- scissors
- stapler

Getting Started with the Mini-Mural

On page 24, you'll find a reproducible mini-mural. This mini-mural fulfills two purposes: 1) It provides an introduction to the theme and 2) it serves as a template for the large bulletin board display. Make a copy of the mini-mural for each child. If necessary, introduce the word *vehicle*. Then ask which of the vehicles children have ridden in. After children tell about their experiences in various kinds of vehicles, proceed with an informal math lesson using stories about the vehicles on the mini-mural. For example:

- The buses and bicycles will all arrive at (your school name). How many vehicles will arrive altogether?
- If you wanted to put 1 bicycle into each van, how many more vans would you need?

Invite children to volunteer their own story problems. Then explain that the class will make a large bulletin board mural like the mini-mural.

Assembling the Math Mural

Follow these steps to create your Transportation bulletin board. You may wish to have students work in groups to prepare the different vehicles (steps 7 and 10) while you prepare the background.

1 Cover the bulletin board with green paper.

2 Cut a strip of light blue paper (wavy on one side and with a straight border on the other) and staple it to the top of the board to create a sky.

3 Cut a piece of dark blue paper and staple it to one corner of the board for an ocean.

4 Cut a strip of brown paper about 1 inch wide and staple it along the bottom of the mural. Draw railroad tracks on this strip.

5 Cut out strips of black paper about $1\frac{1}{2}$ inches wide and staple to the green background to create roads.

6 Duplicate the vehicle patterns on pages 28-32. You may choose to enlarge or reduce the images depending on the size of your bulletin board. I suggest using the following colors and amounts, but you may wish to vary these depending on the ability level of your class and the difficulty of problems that you want to create:

10 cars in different colors
9 trucks in different colors
8 bicycles —2 red, 3 yellow, 3 blue
7 vans in different colors
6 yellow school buses
5 white airplanes
4 gray helicopters
3 white ships
2 gray trains
1 white rocket

7 Have children cut out—and color, if necessary—the vehicles. Suggest that students add details such as windows or company names on the trucks.

8 Staple the vehicles onto the bulletin board either following the arrangement of the mini-mural or using students' suggestions.

9 Duplicate the four border patterns. Note that there is a different pattern for each side of the bulletin board.

10 Instruct children to color the borders as follows:

canoe = gray; horse = brown;
balloon = red and blue

11 Staple the borders along the bulletin board sides.

12 Duplicate the display title on page 27. Ask a volunteer to color the letters before you add it to the mural.

MATH-TO-GO

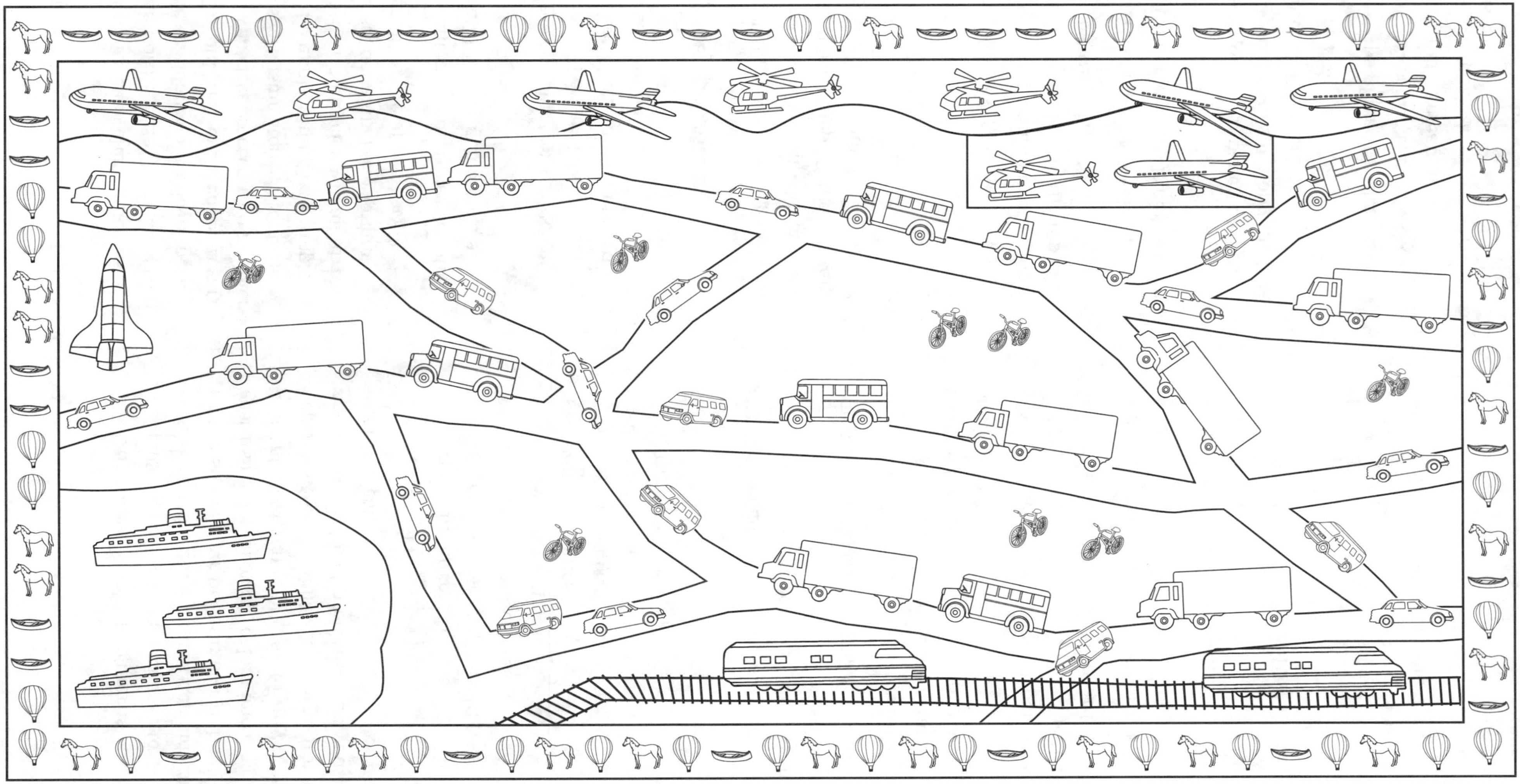

Using the Transportation Math Mural

You'll find that this math mural has many uses. You might begin by giving children problems such as the ones shown here. Then encourage them to make up their own problems. You'll also want to assign the reproducible worksheets on pages 34-37.

Sample Story Problems

- Are there more buses or cars?
- How many helicopters and airplanes are there? Are there any other vehicles that can fly? How many kinds of vehicles can fly? How many vehicles can fly altogether?

Sample Pattern Problems

- How many different things to ride on are in this pattern?
- Give each kind of picture a number. What is the number pattern for this border?

Sample Estimation Problems

- Estimate how many times this pattern repeats itself. Count to check.
- Estimate how many of each picture are on one of the borders.
- Count to check. How many of each picture are on all the borders? Count to check.

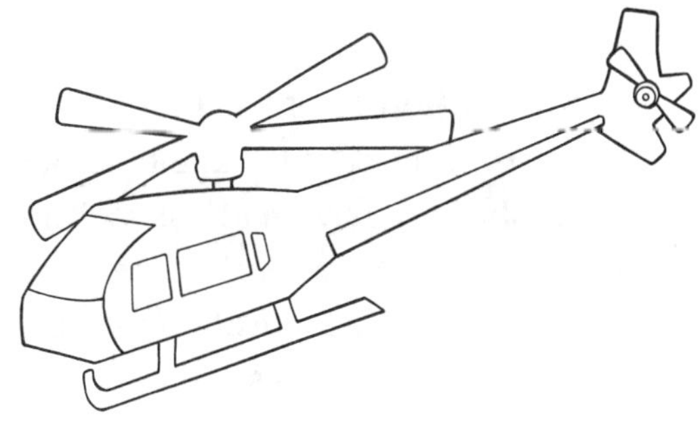

Measuring

Suggest that children name the streets on the mural. Then provide tape measures and have them work with partners to determine the length of each street or the distance between specific vehicles.

Multiplication

The transportation unit is a good place for beginning multiplication. For example, after discussing how many wheels a bicycle has, have children figure out how many bicycle wheels there are in all. Continue with cars (4 wheels), trucks (6 wheels), and trains (12 wheels).

Using the Worksheets

Provide children with pages 34-37. You might wish to have them team up with partners to check one another's work.

Adding Ways To Go

Explain that children should write number problems to match the pictures on the math mural. For example, for the first problem they would write 5 (airplanes) plus 4 (helicopters). Students should then complete the addition. Conclude by asking them how they can check their work.

Subtracting Ways To Go

Have children use the math mural to write the number equations for this page as well.

Transportation Graphing

Students can use this page to make a graph showing how many of each kind of vehicle are on the mural. Once the graphs are completed, ask questions such as:

- How many bicycles are there?
- How many more cars are there than vans?

Transportation Questions

Have children use the data on the math mural to complete this page. Note that questions 6 and 7 involve measuring.

Cross-Curricular Activities

Language Arts

- Collect fiction and nonfiction books about transportation to place in a reading corner. If you have multiple copies of a book, set up small groups to read them. You might have children read to answer specific questions.
- Have children prepare pictorial or written reports about a vehicle of their choice.
- Compile a list of new vocabulary words that relate to transportation. Have children alphabetize the list.

Social Studies

- Visit a local transportation center—an airport or train or bus station. You might also visit a museum to see vehicles from the past.
- Invite a local merchant in to talk to children about why transportation is important to his or her business. Or ask a transportation worker such as a school bus driver to talk to the class about his or her job.

Art

- Have children work together to create a pictograph of how they travel to school each day.
- Encourage children to create fanciful vehicles from plastic building materials such as Lego™.

Music

- Teach children transportation-related songs such as "The Wheels of the Bus Go Round and Round" or "Row, Row, Row Your Boat."

Literature Links

- *Young Amelia Earhart* by Susan Alcott
- *The Big Balloon Race* by Carolyn Croll
- *Clipper Ship* by Thomas P. Lewis
- *The Little Engine That Could* by Watty Piper
- *Grandfather's Journey* by Allen Say
- *Young Orville and Wilbur Wright* by Andrew Woods

Oceans of Math: Reproducible Page

Use these letter patterns to name your math board. With the help of a Xerox copier you can enlarge each letter even more!

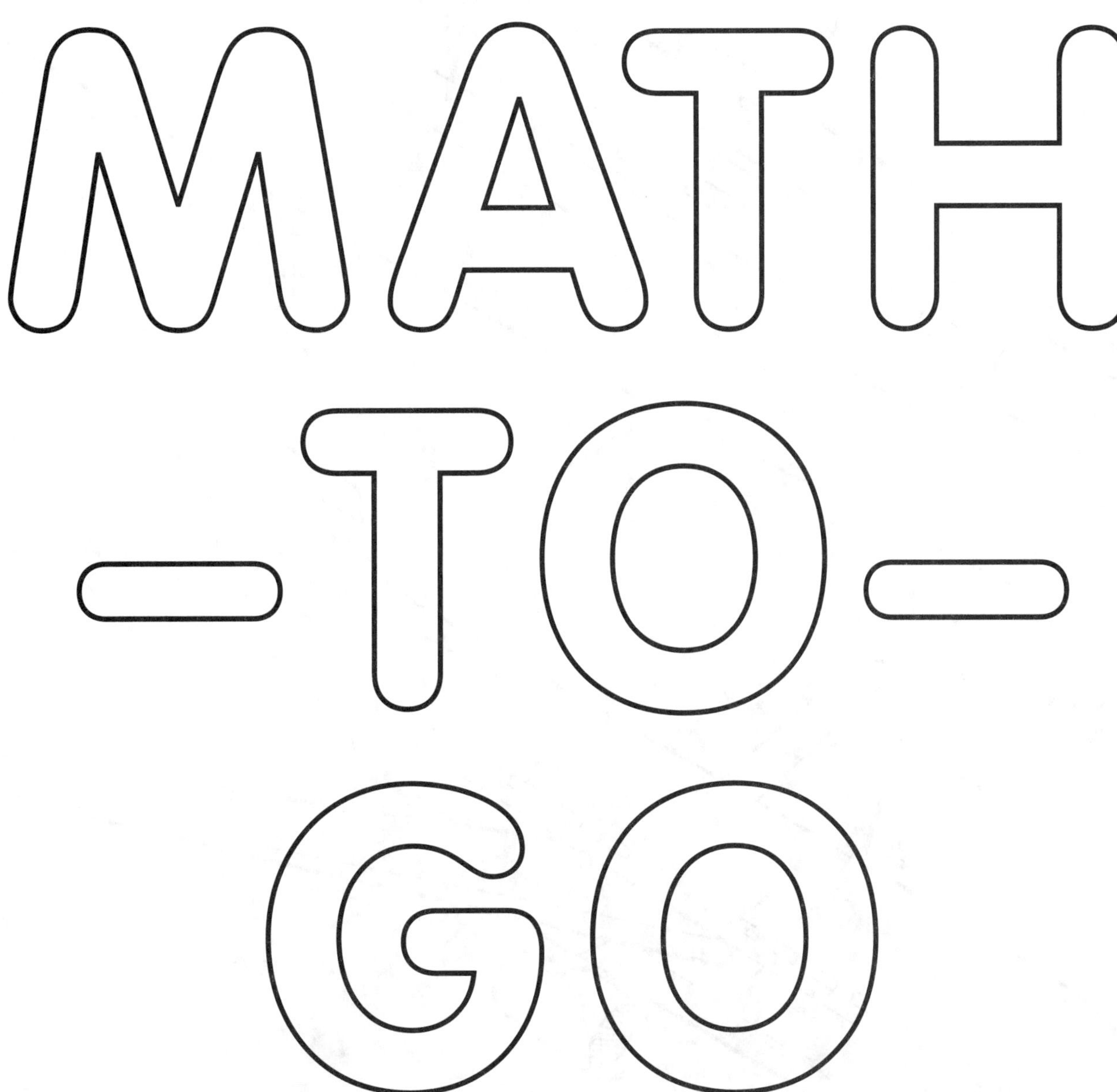

Math-To-Go: Reproducible Page

Copy on white paper. The numbers in parentheses suggest how many you will need of each pattern.

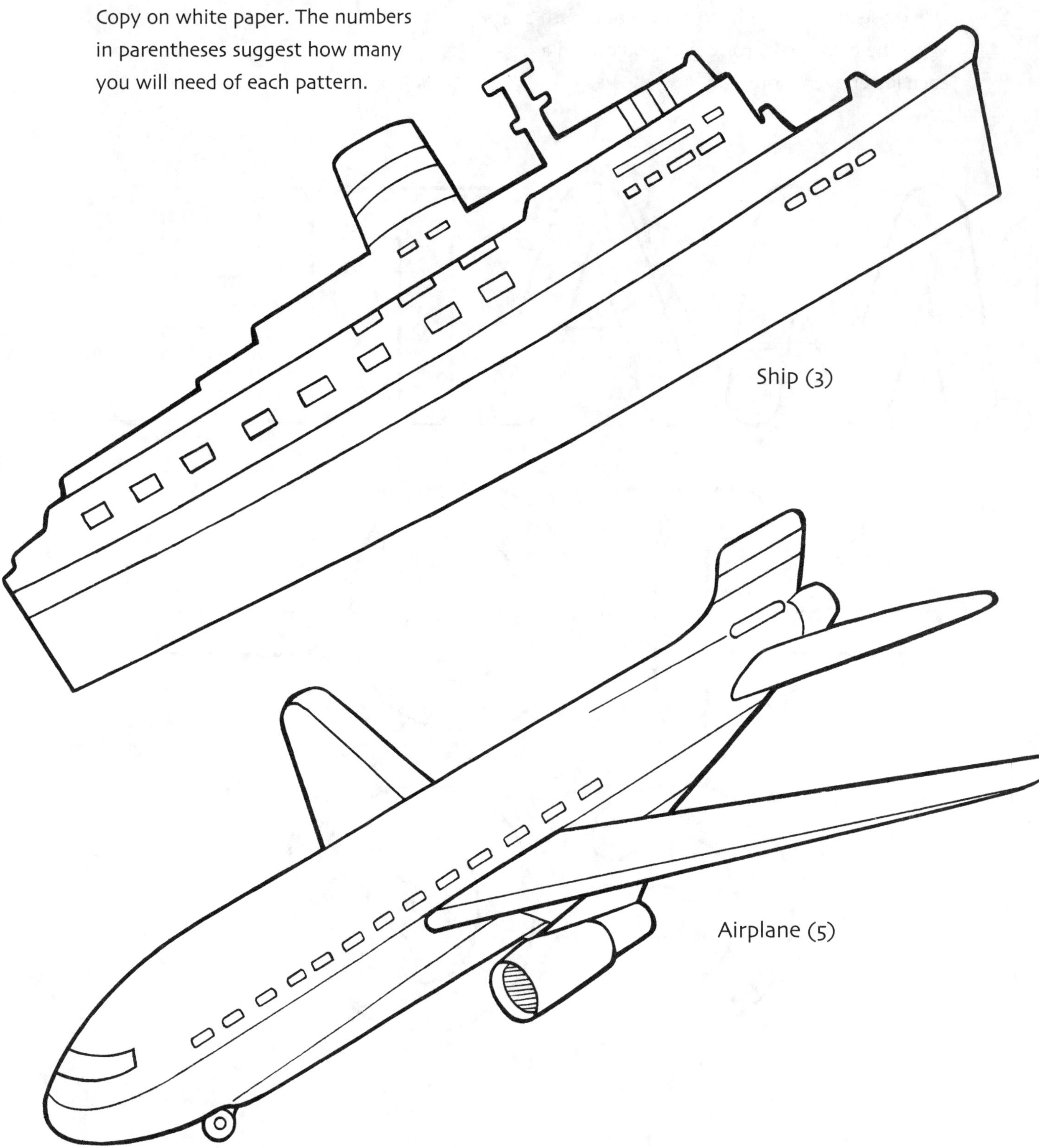

Ship (3)

Airplane (5)

Math-To-Go: Reproducible Page

Copy on gray paper. The numbers in parentheses suggest how many you will need of each pattern.

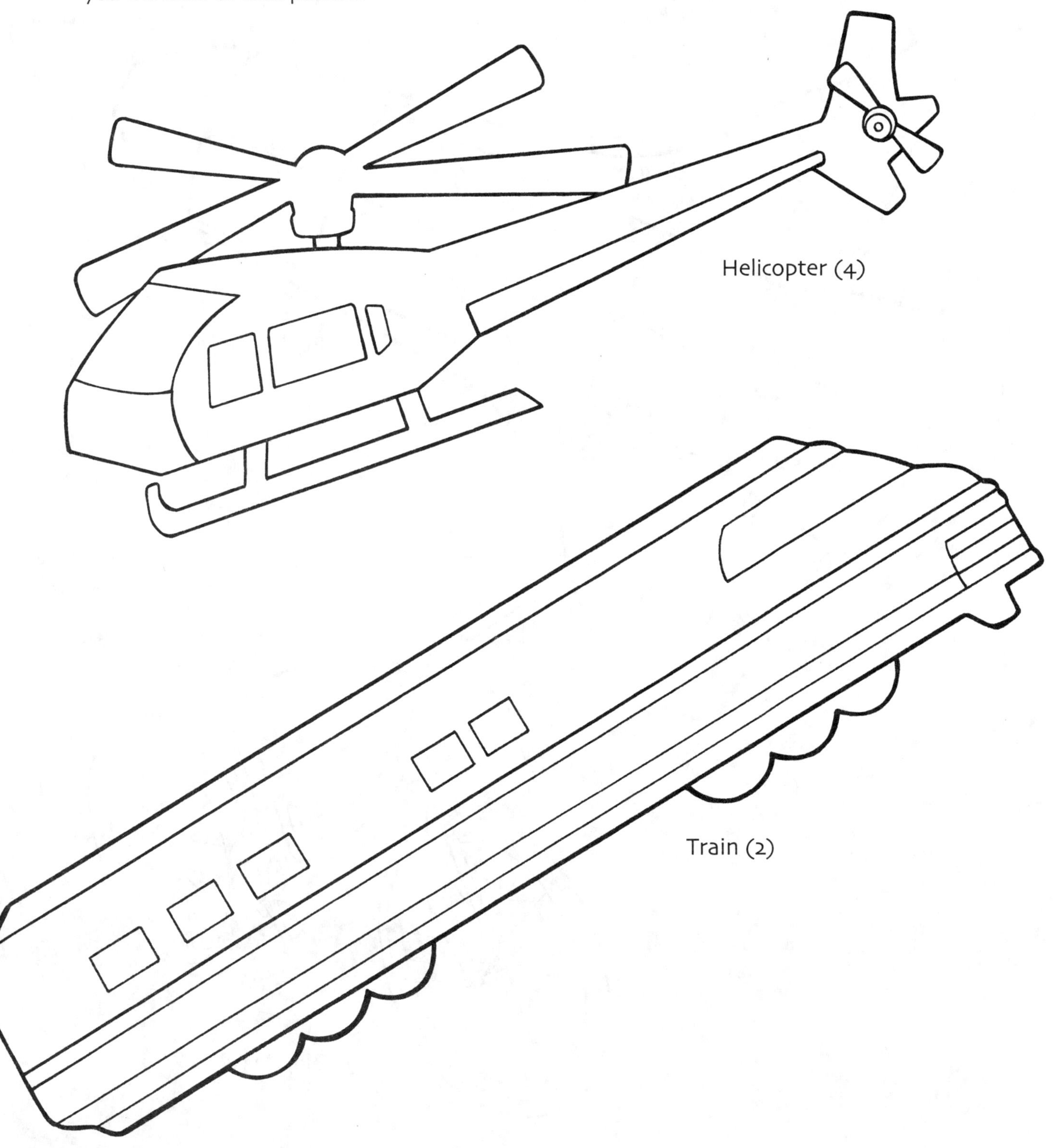

Math-To-Go: Reproducible Page

Copy on white paper. The numbers in parentheses suggest how many you will need of each pattern. Have children color the bicycles as described on page 23.

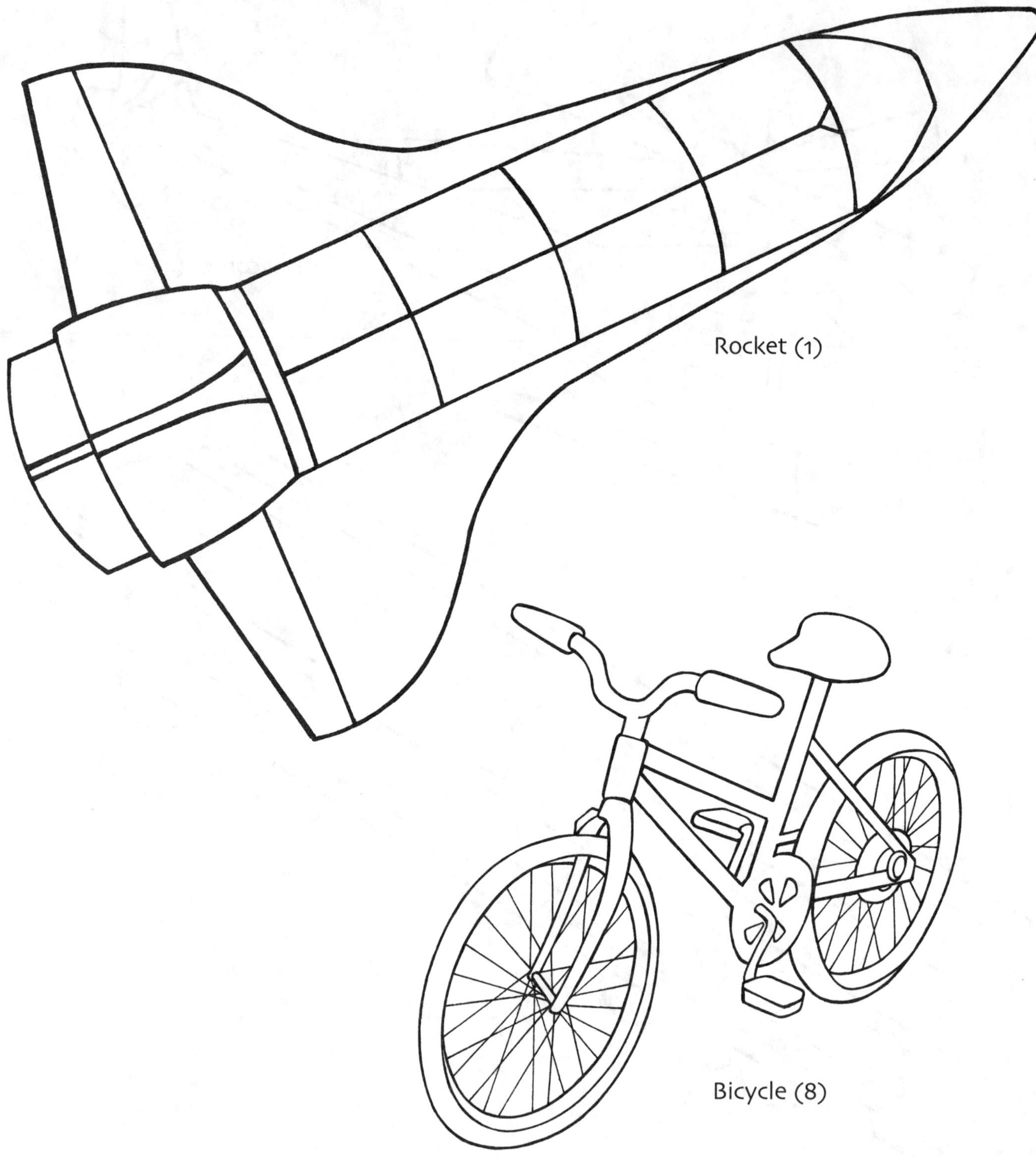

Rocket (1)

Bicycle (8)

Math-To-Go: Reproducible Page

Copy on white paper. The numbers in parentheses suggest how many you will need of each pattern. Have children color the vehicles in different colors.

Car (10)

Van (7)

Math-To-Go: Reproducible Page

Copy on white paper. The numbers in parentheses suggest how many you will need of each pattern. Have children color the vehicles as described on page 23.

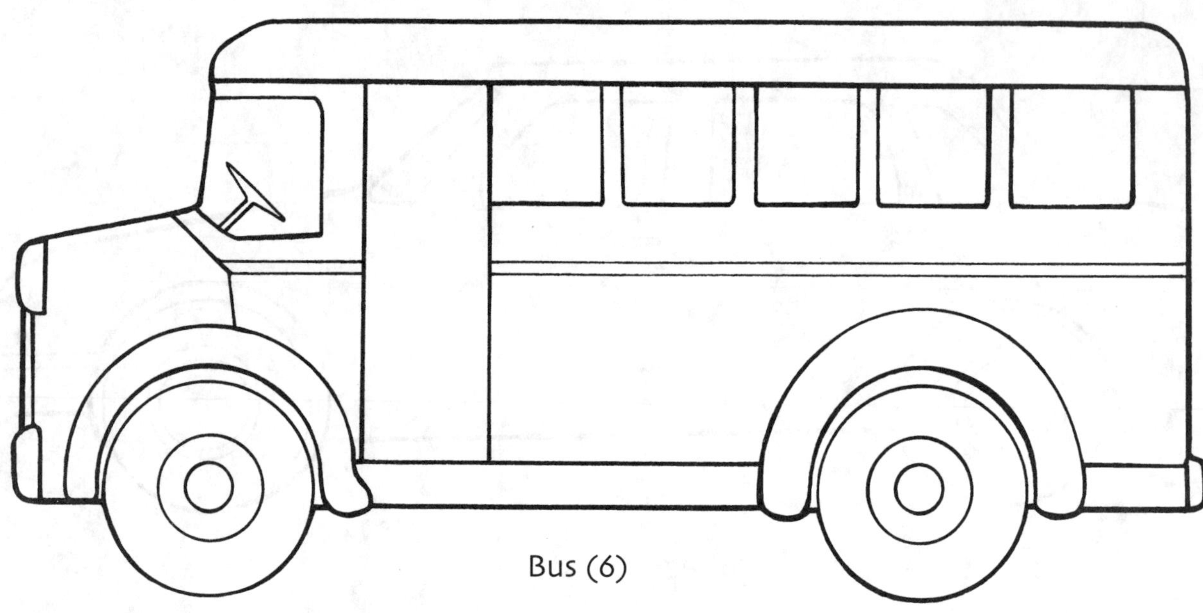

Bus (6)

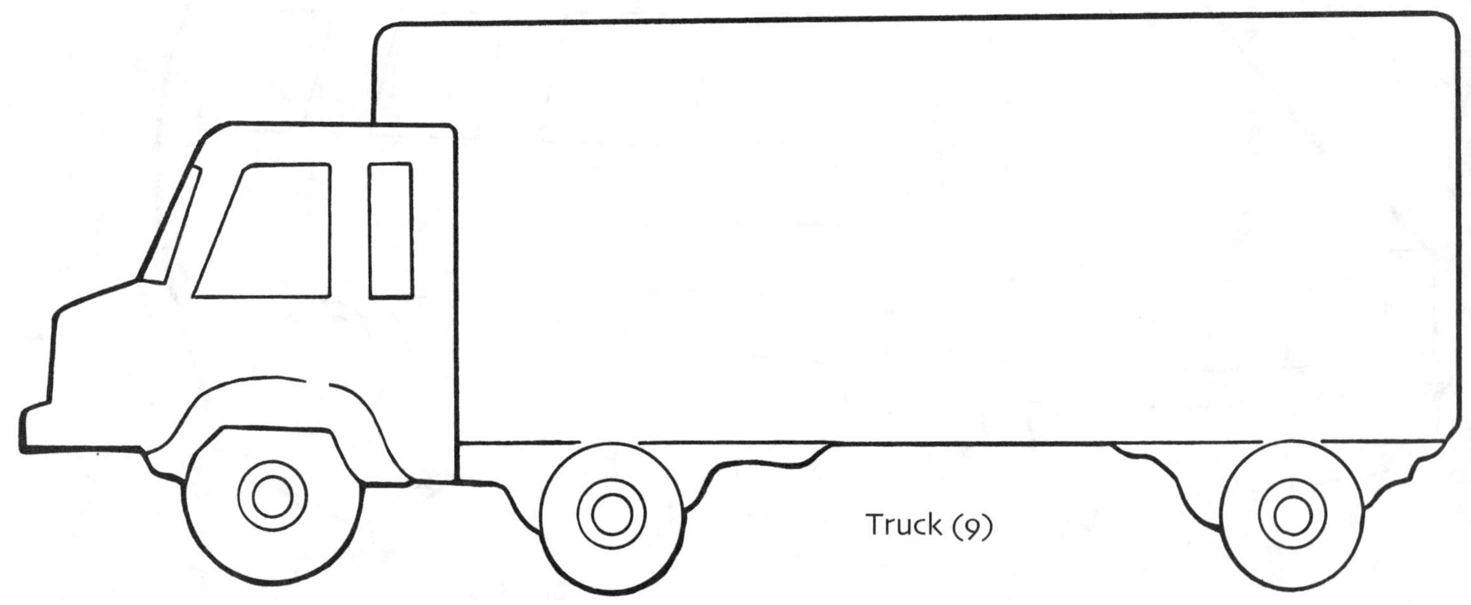

Truck (9)

Math-To-Go: Reproducible Page Copy the border patterns on white or manila paper. Have children color them as suggested on page 23.

Top Border	Bottom Border	Right Border	Left Border

Name: ______________________________

Adding Ways To Go

Use the math mural to write the numbers in the squares.
Add the numbers.

1.

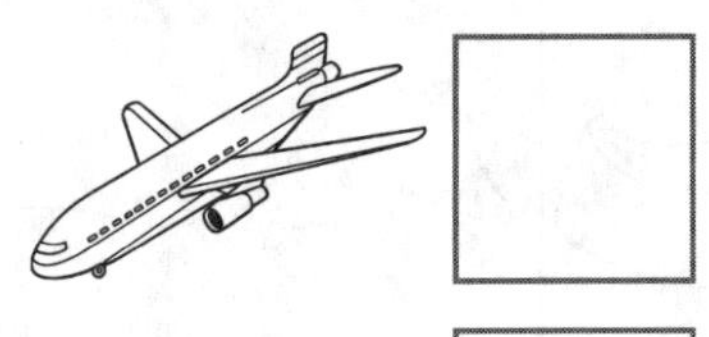

\+

2.

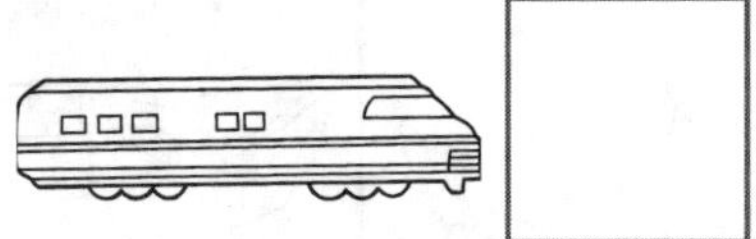

\+

3.

\+

4.

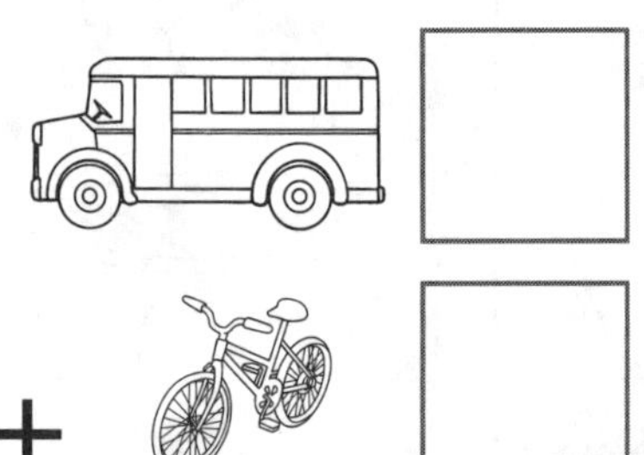

\+

5.

\+

6.

\+

7.

\+

8.

\+

9.

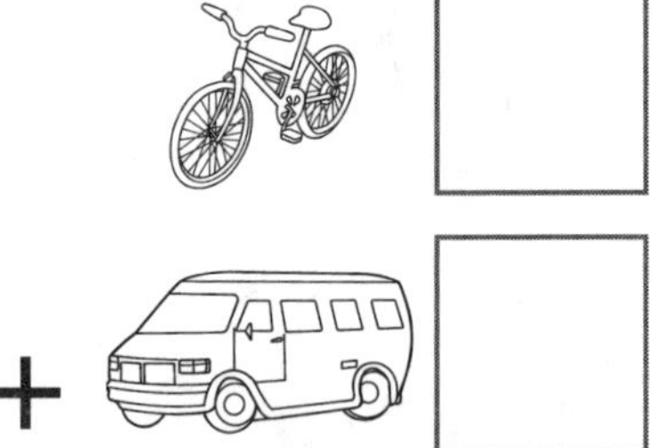

\+

Name: ______________________________

Subtracting Ways To Go

Use the math mural to write the numbers in the squares.
Subtract the numbers.

1.

2.

3.

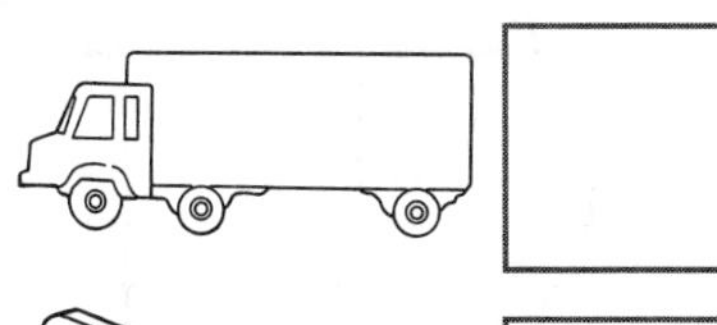

4.

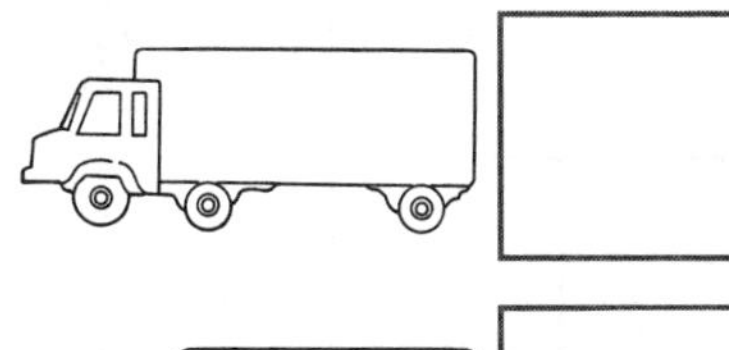

5.

6.

7.

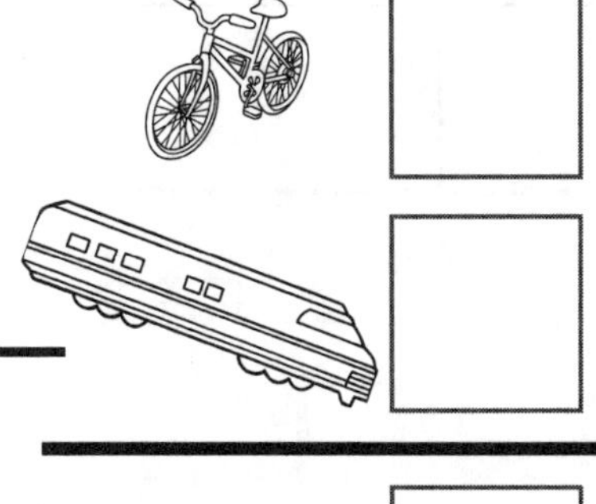

8.

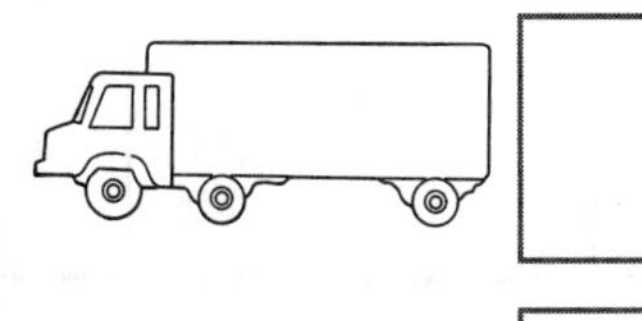

9.

Name: ______________________________

Transportation Graphing

Use the math mural to count the different ways to travel.
Color the graph to show how many of each picture you count.

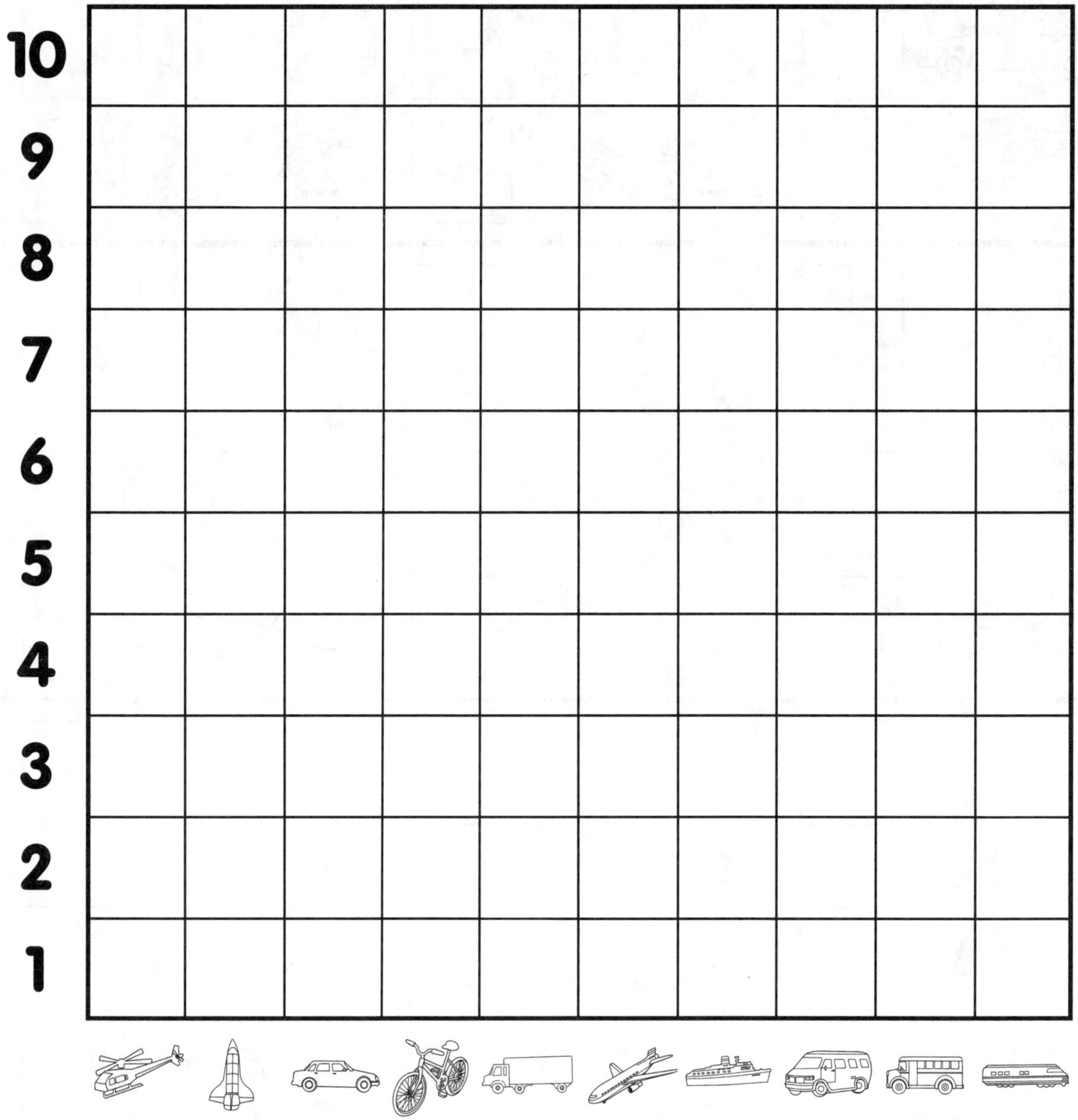

10										
9										
8										
7										
6										
5										
4										
3										
2										
1										

Name: ______________________________

Transportation Questions

Use the math mural to answer the questions.

1. How many planes and copters are there in all? ____________

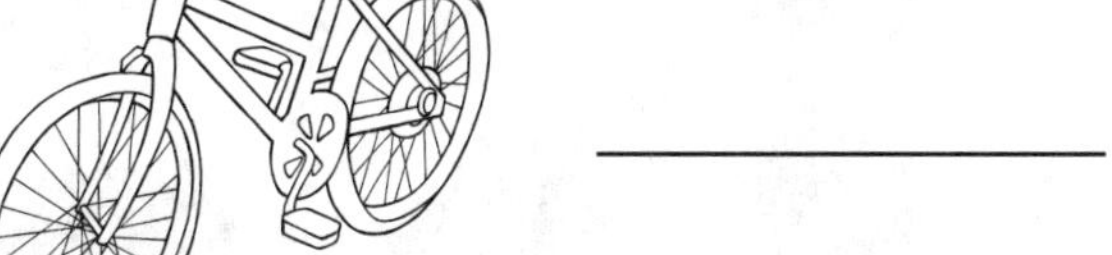

2. How many more cars are there than bikes? ____________

3. If all of the cars and vans went to your town, how many parking spaces would be needed? ____________

4. There are 2 people in each truck. How many people are in the trucks? ____________

5. If there are 5 children on each bus, how many children in all are riding a bus to school? ____________

6. How many inches long is a car? ____________

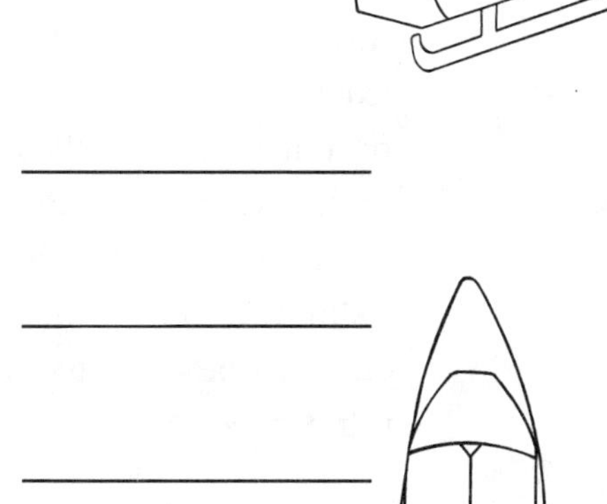

7. How many centimeters long is a train? ____________

Challenge! Each copter picks up 2 people on the way to the city and 5 people on the way back. How many people are picked up in all? ____________

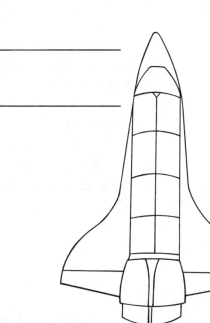

Crawling with Math

Talking About the Theme: Insects

Many children love to observe insects, and even those who are squeamish about them will be able to satisfy their curiosity via a math mural.

After assembling this mural, I suggest leaving it up for several weeks both to practice math skills and to expand children's knowledge about the theme. Keep in mind, though, the length of time for using the Insect bulletin board is flexible and can be adjusted for your own scheduling needs.

Materials

Before flying into this theme, you'll want to collect materials for assembling the bulletin board. You'll need:

- insect patterns on pages 44-48
- border patterns on page 49
- roll of brown craft paper
- roll of light blue craft paper
- light green, black, yellow, tan, and white construction paper
- crayons or colored markers
- scissors
- stapler

Getting Started with the Mini-Mural

The Insect mini-mural on page 40 is an excellent way to introduce the theme. It also provides a template for you to follow when placing the insects on the large math mural.

Make a copy of the mini-mural for each child. Identify and discuss each insect. Then proceed with an informal math lesson by presenting stories about the insects. For example:

- How many flies and butterflies are there altogether?
- If 4 of the water bugs crawl out of the water, how many are left in the water?

Ask students to volunteer their own story problems. Then explain that they will be helping you to create a large bulletin board mural similar to the mini-mural.

Assembling the Math Mural

Follow these steps to create your Insects bulletin board. You may wish to have students work in groups to prepare the different insects (steps 6 and 9) while you complete the mural background.

1 Cover the top part (about $^1/_4$ of the bulletin board) with light blue craft paper to make the sky.

2 Cover the remaining $^3/_4$ of the bulletin board with brown craft paper to make the ground. Cut small hills at the top.

3 Cut out a blue construction paper pond and add it to the board.

4 Cut out green paper grass and weeds (about 6 inches high) to place around the pond and on the ground.

5 Duplicate the insect patterns on pages 44-48. You may choose to enlarge or reduce the images depending on the size of your bulletin board. I recommend the following colors and amounts:

10 dark gray ants
9 brown water bugs
8 tan fireflies
7 orange monarch butterflies
6 yellow bees with brown wings
5 red ladybugs with black spots
4 light green praying mantises with brown undersides
3 dark gray flies
2 light green luna moths
1 green grasshopper

6 Have students cut out and color the insects.

7 Staple the insects onto the background according to the mini-mural arrangement or your own design.

BOARD TIP

When stapling the flying insects, staple their bodies and fold the wings outward to give a three-dimensional look. Also fold some of the blades of grass and weeds outward and place some of the insects on the blades.

8 Duplicate the border patterns on page 49 on light green or yellow paper. Note that there is a different pattern for each side of the mural.

9 Have students color the border insects as follows:

mosquitoes = black
dragonflies = blue
fruit flies = tan

Staple the borders along the bulletin board.

10 Duplicate the display title on page 43. Invite volunteers to color it before you add it to the mural.

CRAWLING WITH MATH

Using the Insects Bulletin Board

You can use the insect math mural to give students practice in counting, addition, subtraction, multiplication, graphing, measuring, word problems, patterns, and estimation. Begin by giving the class problems such as these, then encourage students to make up their own. You'll also want to use the reproducible worksheets on pages 50-53.

Sample Story Problems

- 4 bees buzz off to their hive. How many bees are left?
- The luna moths visit the water bugs. How many insects are in the pond?

Sample Pattern Problems

- How many dragonflies are in this pattern? How many mosquitoes?
- What insect comes next in this pattern? How many of this insect do you need to complete this part of the pattern?

Sample Estimation

- Estimate how many dragonflies are on the left border? Check your guess.

Using the Worksheets

As students begin to make up their own math problems based on the bulletin board, provide them with the reproducible pages for this unit.

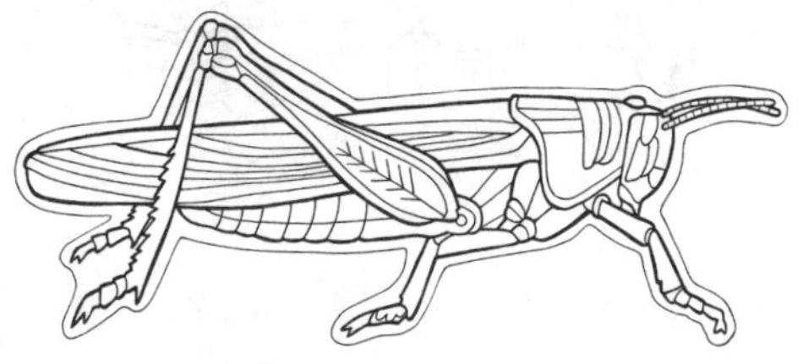

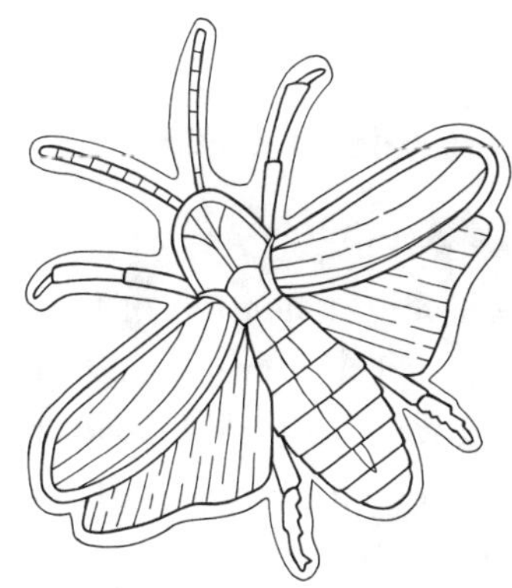

Insect Addition

Remind students that they should write number problems to match the pictures on the bulletin board. For example, for the first problem, students would write 2 luna moths and 3 flies. Students should then complete the addition and check their work.

Insect Subtraction

For this page, students again use the bulletin board to determine the number of insects for each problem.

Insect Graphing

Have children use this page to make a graph showing how many of each insect there are on the math mural. Children can use their completed graphs to make up questions. Model examples such as:

- Which column has the most colored squares? Why?
- Which column has the fewest colored squares? Why?
- How many insects are there in all? How did you use the graph to find out?

Insect Questions

Have children use the bulletin board to answer the questions on this page. Note that addition, subtraction, multiplication, estimation, counting by 2's, and measurement are all required.

Cross-Curricular Activities

Language Arts

- Assemble a collection of books, both fiction and nonfiction, about insects. Place these on a table and invite children to learn more about the insects on the math mural.
- Have students write poems or stories about an insect. Tell students to include one or two interesting facts in their piece.

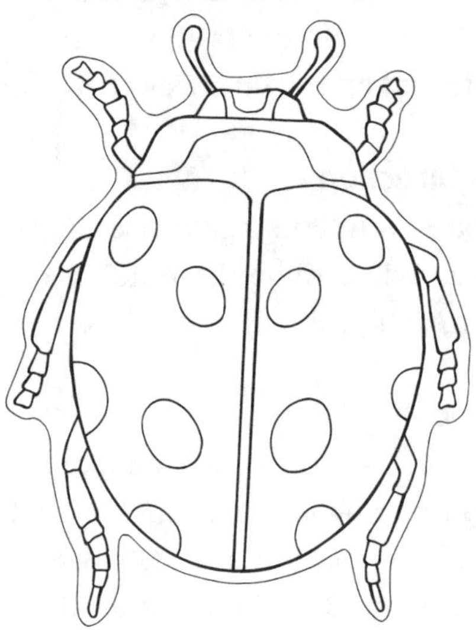

Art

- Children might make insects from scrap materials such as egg cartons, pipe cleaners, gauze, coffee filters, felt, clay, toothpicks, or tissue paper. Have children label their insects and write a descriptive sentence about them. Set up a classroom display for all to enjoy.
- Have children use the patterns on pages 44-49 to make paper insects for a mobile. With different lengths of yarn, hang the insects from wire hangers.

Science

- Equip children with insect jars so that they can catch, observe, and write about the real thing. Be sure children understand the importance of returning their insects to nature.
- Take a nature walk to observe where insects live. Bring along magnifying glasses.
- Study the life cycles of various insects.
- Work with the class to draw and label the different parts of an insect.

Literature Links

- *The Very Quiet Cricket* and *The Very Hungry Caterpillar* by Eric Carle
- *Where Butterflies Grow* by Joanne Ryder
- *The Icky Bug Alphabet Book* by Jerry Pallotta
- *Bugs* by Nancy Winslow Parker and Joan Richards Wright
- *Two Bad Ants* by Chris Van Allsburg

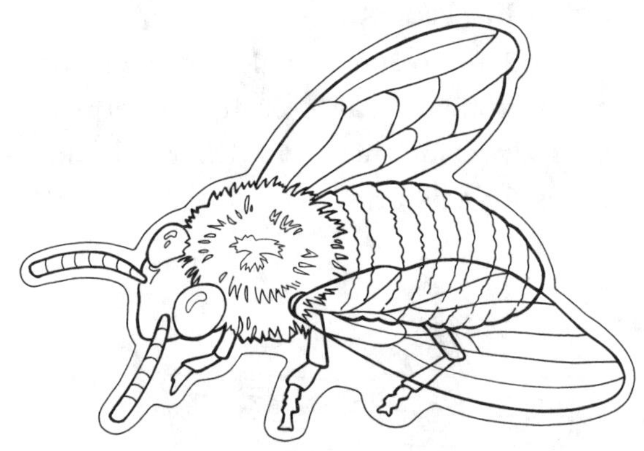

Crawling with Math: Reproducible Page

Use these letter patterns to name your math board. With the help of a Xerox copier you can enlarge each letter even more!

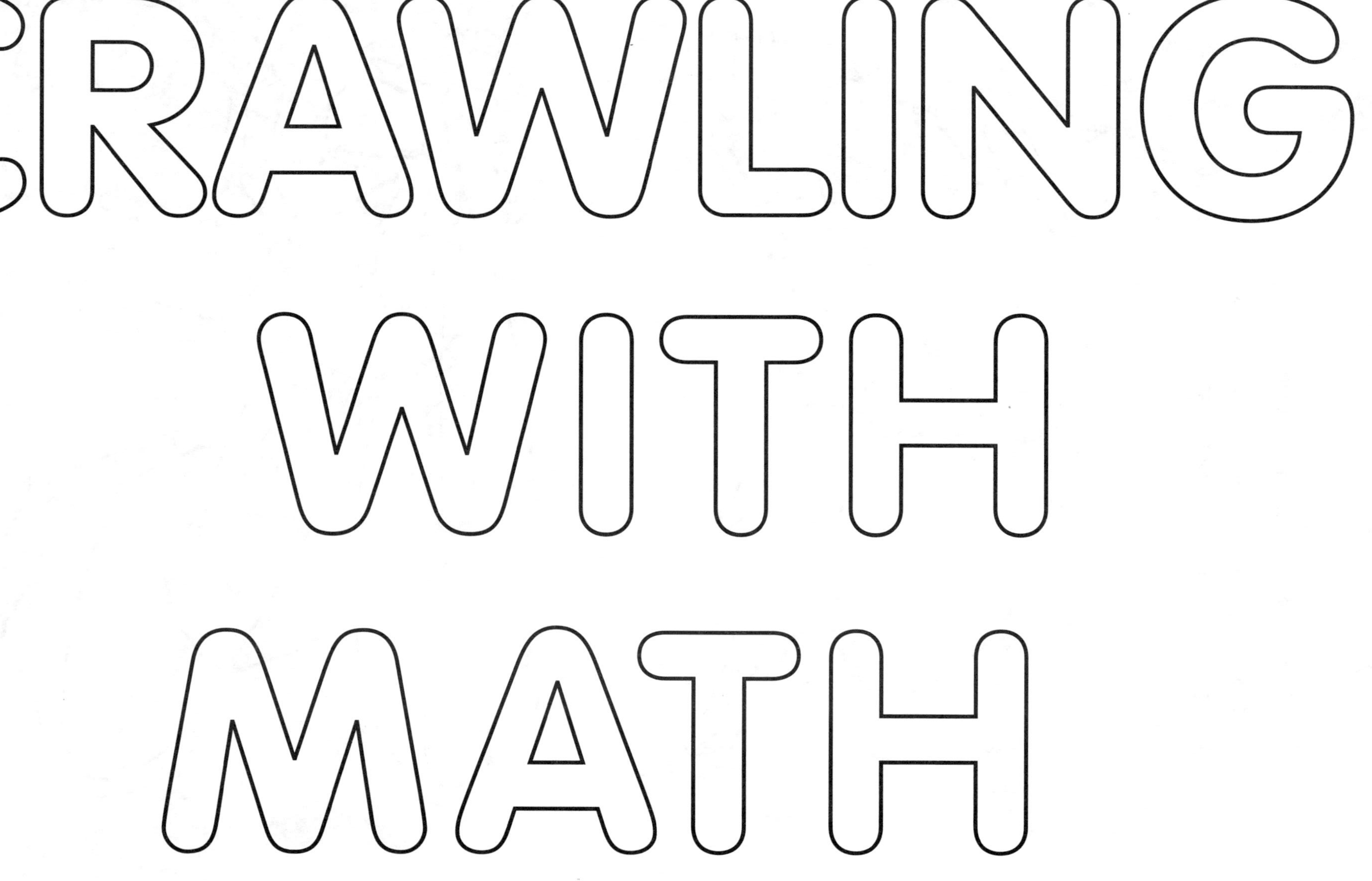

Crawling With Math: Reproducible Page

Copy on dark gray paper. The numbers in parentheses suggest how many you will need of each pattern.

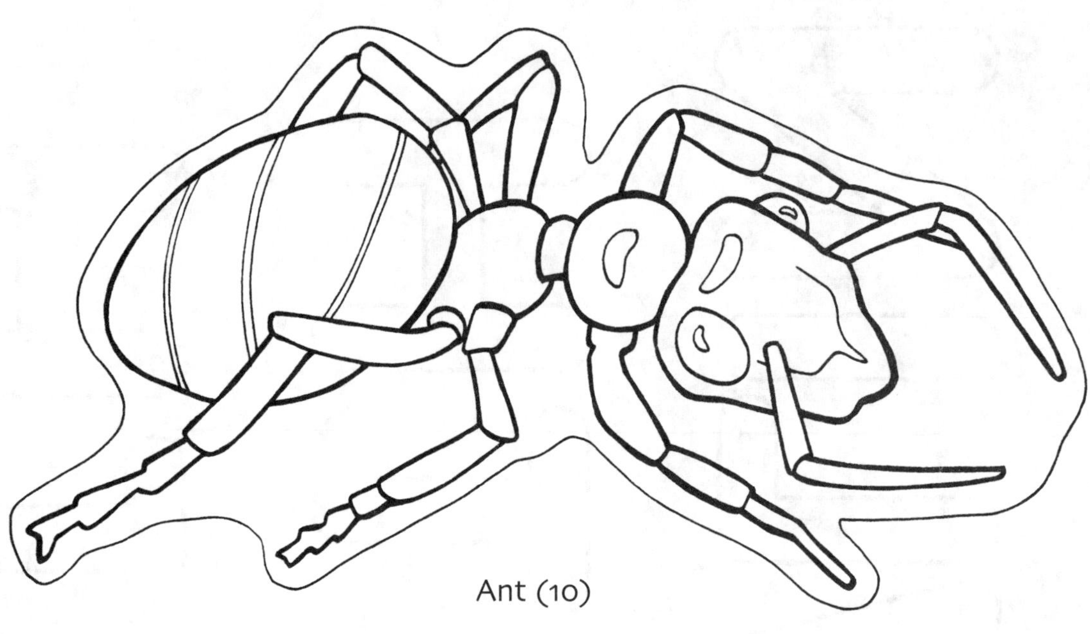

Ant (10)

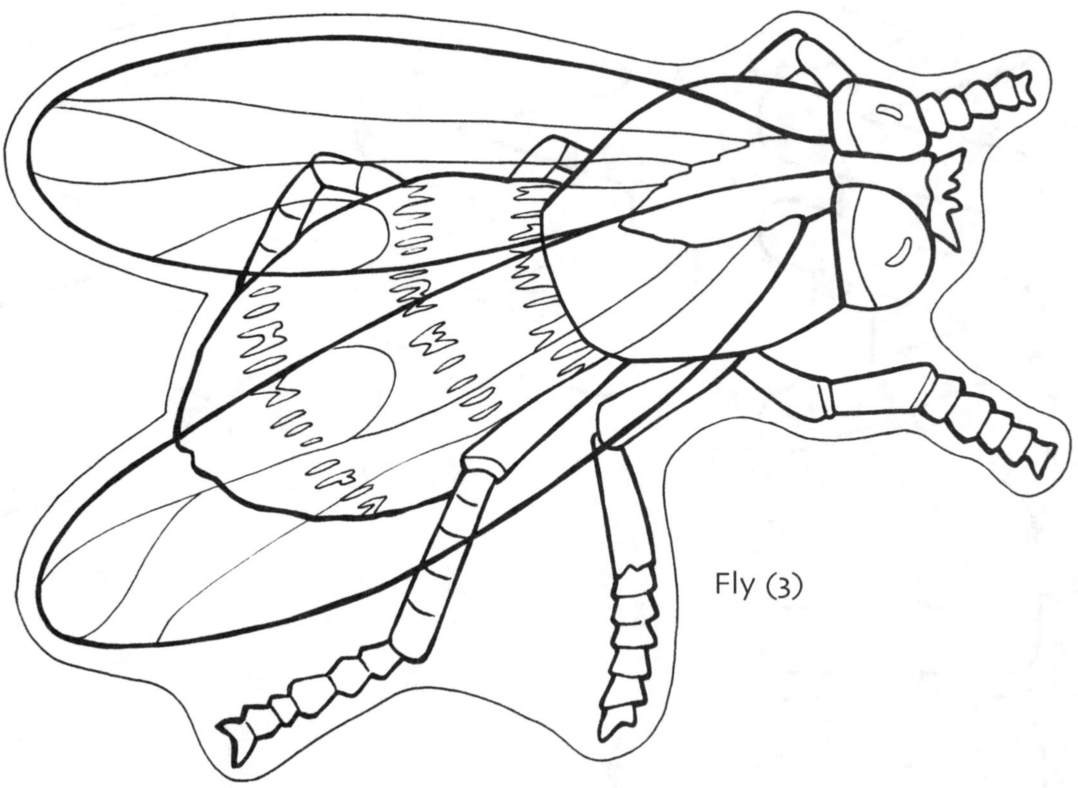

Fly (3)

Crawling With Math: Reproducible Page

Copy on light green paper. The numbers in parentheses suggest how many you will need of each pattern. Have children color the lower side of the praying mantis brown.

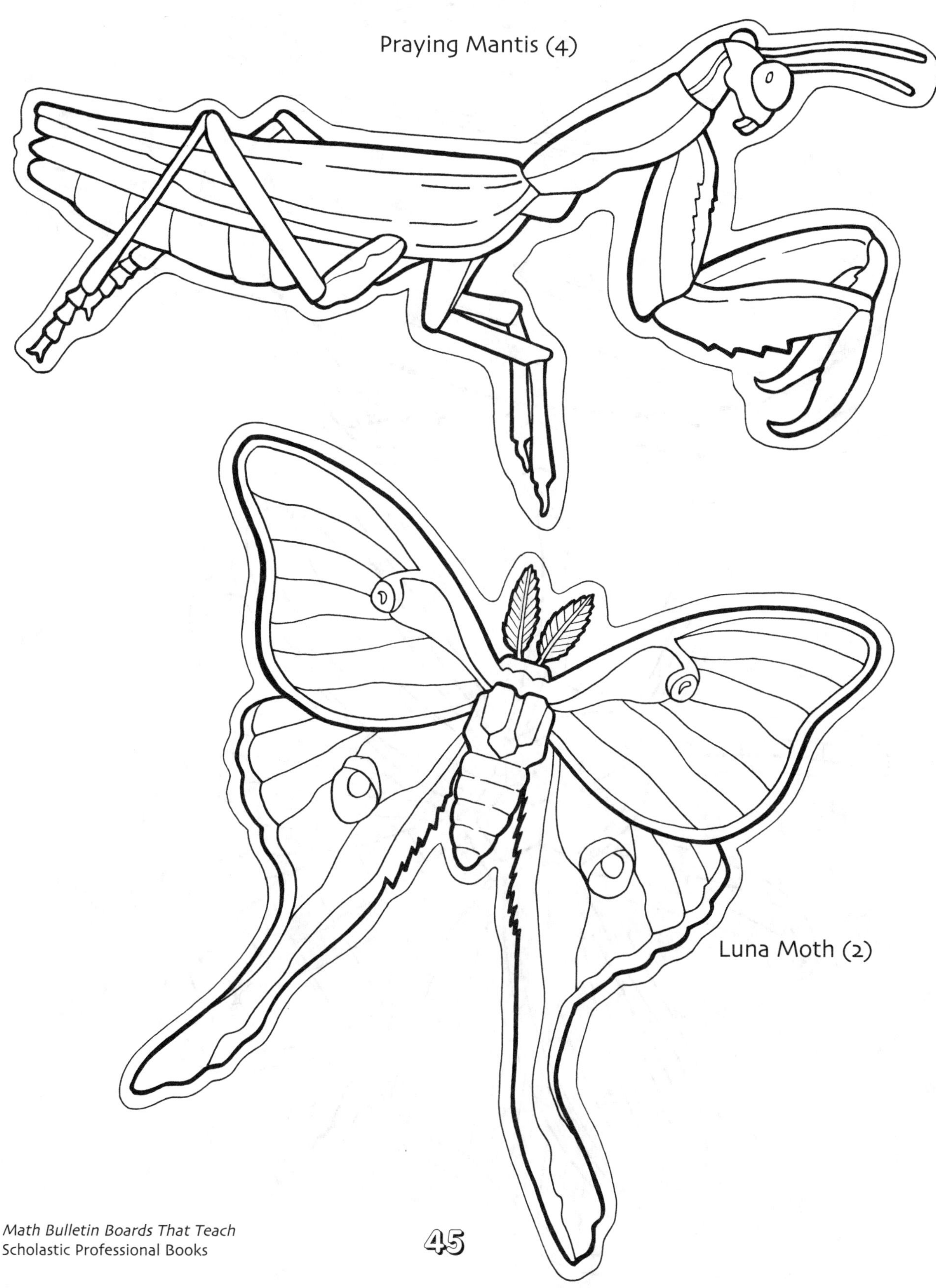

Crawling With Math: Reproducible Page

Copy on tan paper. The numbers in parentheses suggest how many you will need of each pattern. Have children color the water bugs brown.

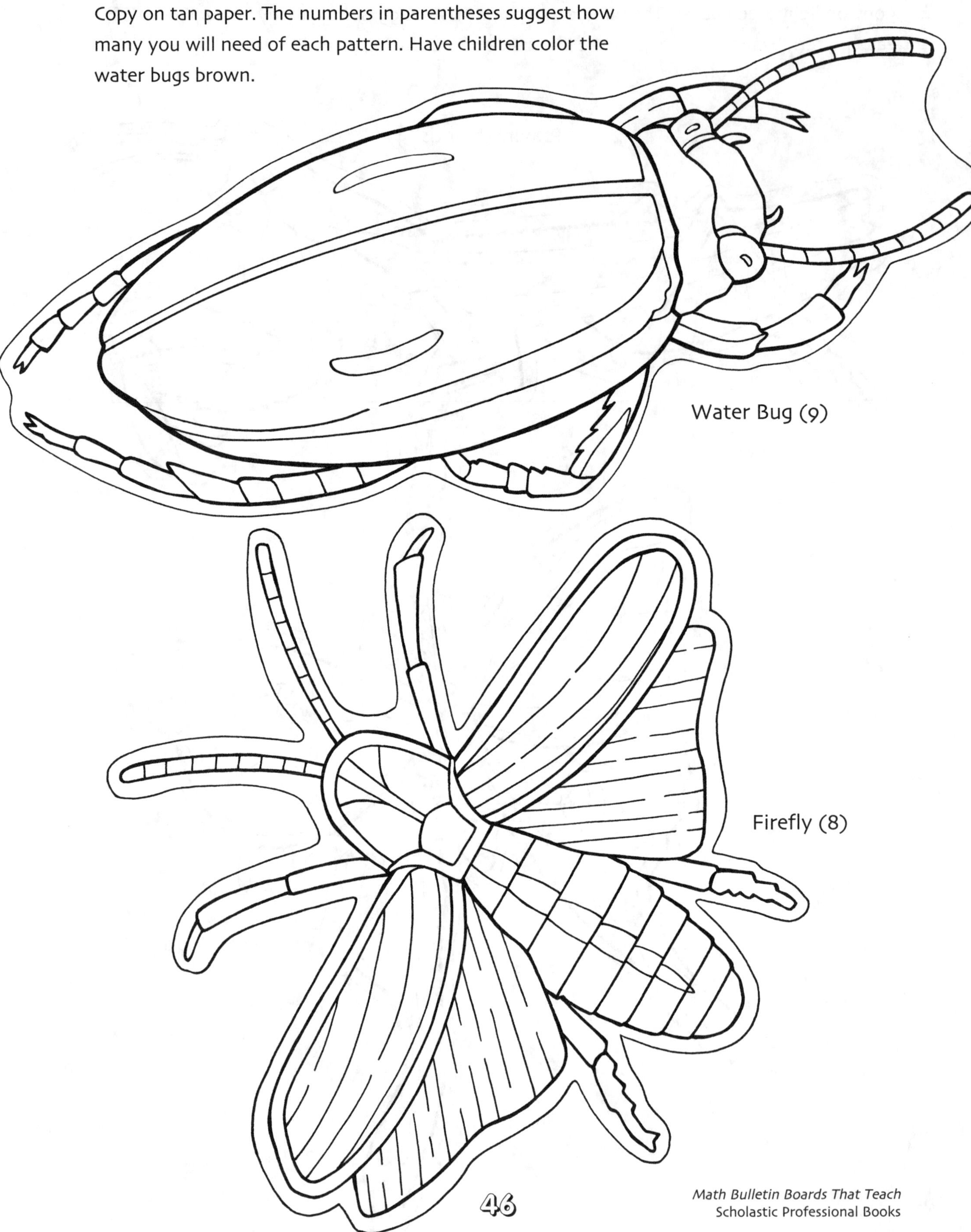

Crawling With Math: Reproducible Page

Copy on yellow paper. The numbers in parentheses suggest how many you will need of each pattern. Have children color the butterflies orange.

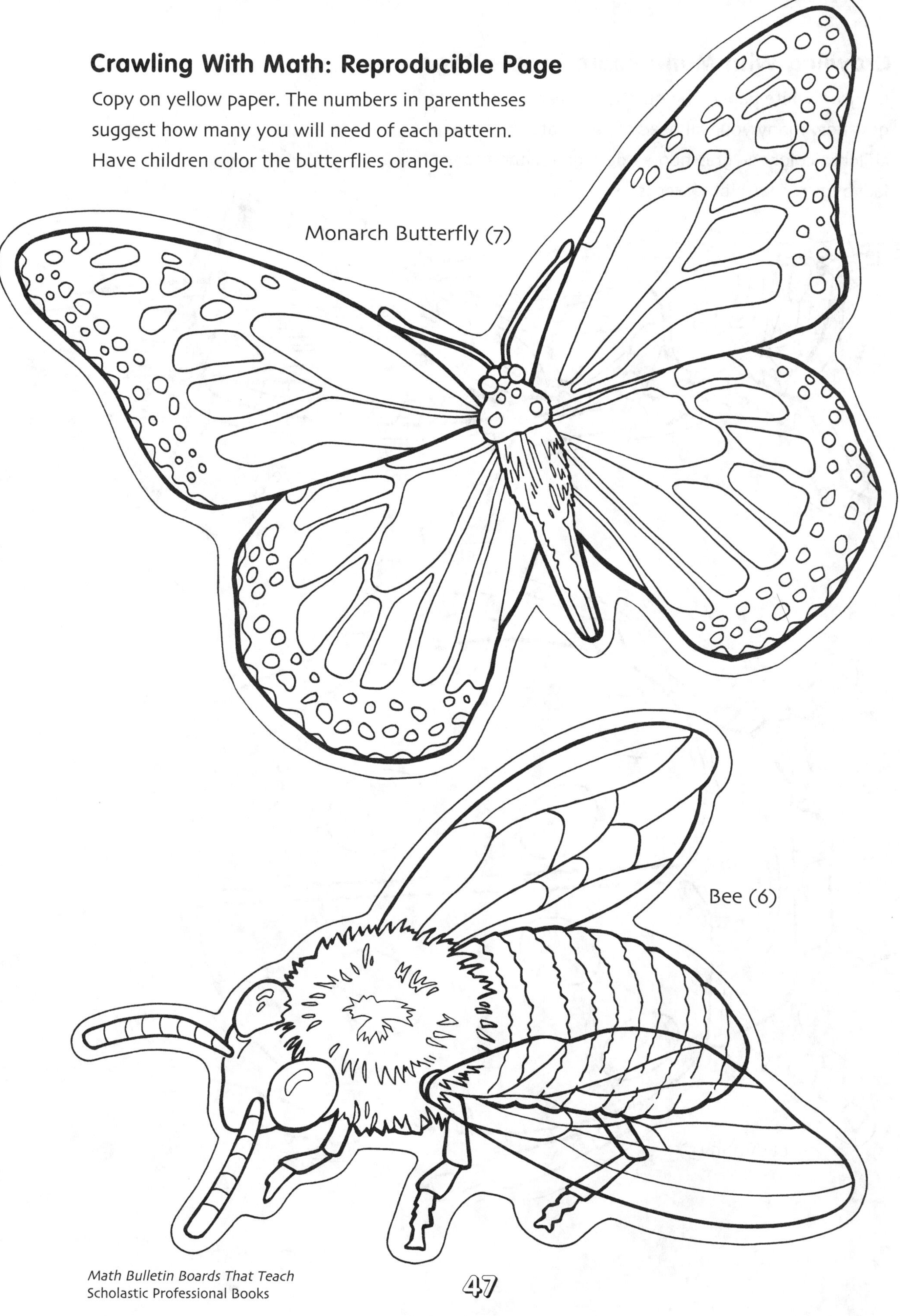

Crawling With Math: Reproducible Page

Copy on white paper. The numbers in parentheses suggest how many you will need of each pattern. Have children color the grasshopper dark green and the ladybugs red with black spots.

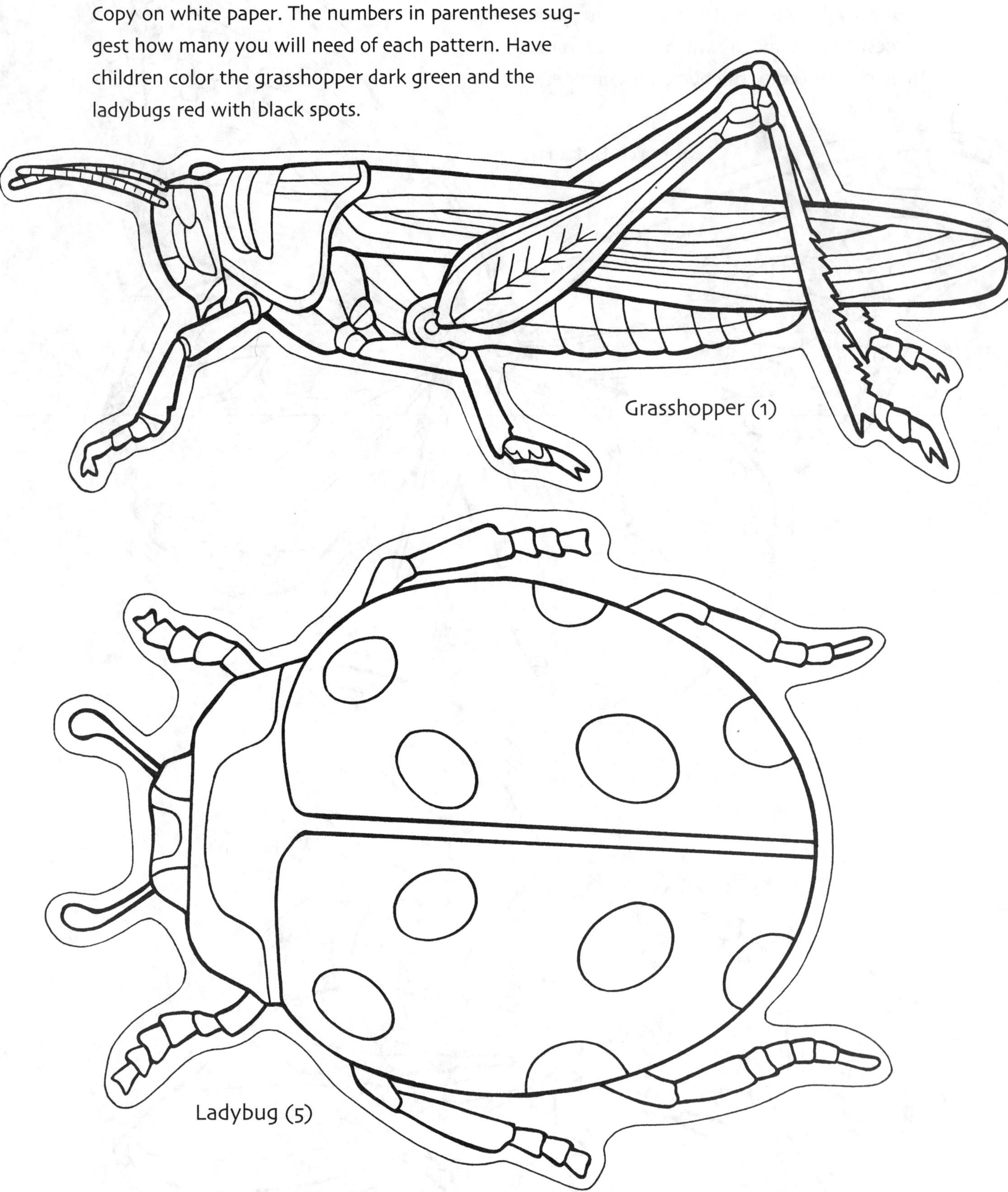

Crawling With Math: Reproducible Page Copy the border patterns on white paper. Have children color them as suggested on page 39.

Top Border	Bottom Border	Right Border	Left Border

Name: ______________________________

Insect Addition

Use the math mural to write the numbers in the squares.
Add the numbers.

1.

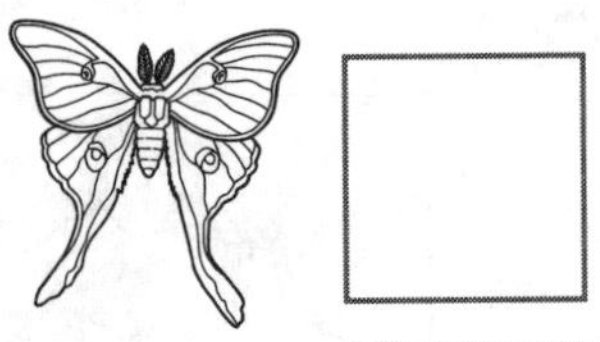

\+

2.

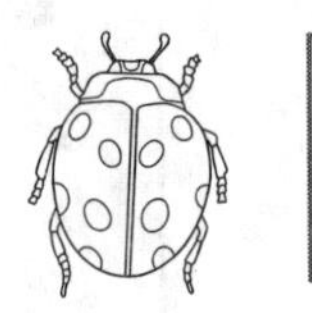

\+

3.

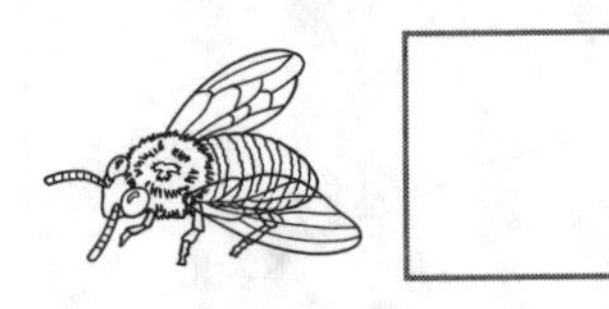

\+

4.

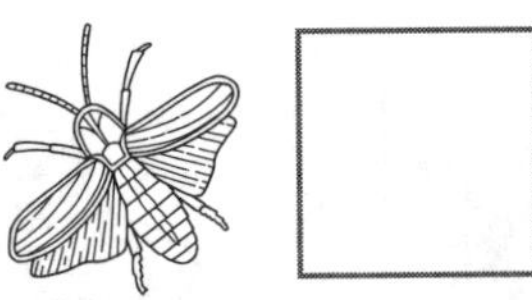

\+

5.

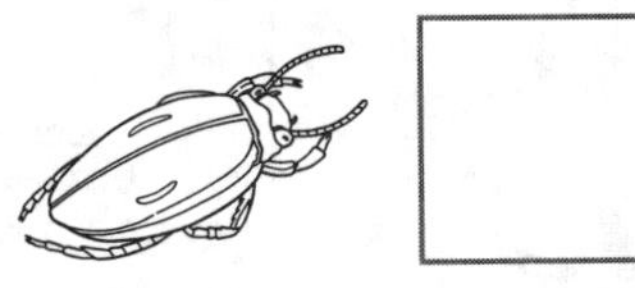

\+

6.

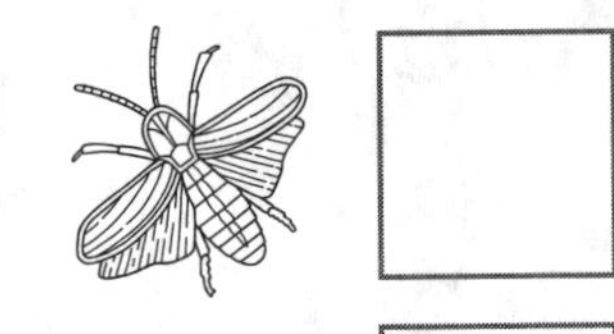

\+

7.

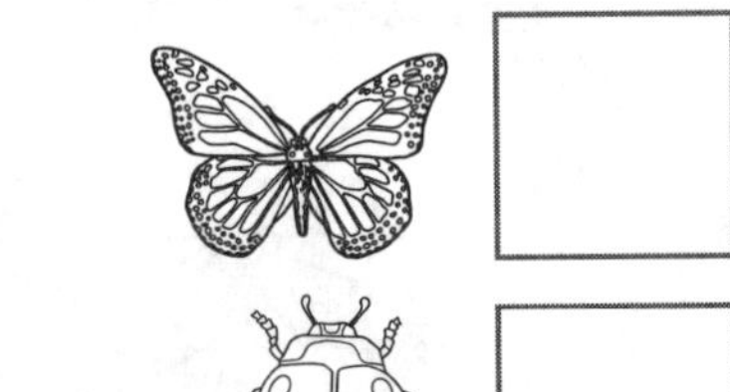

\+

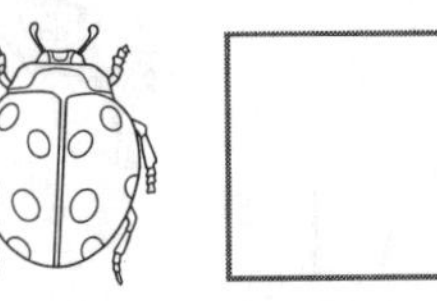

8.

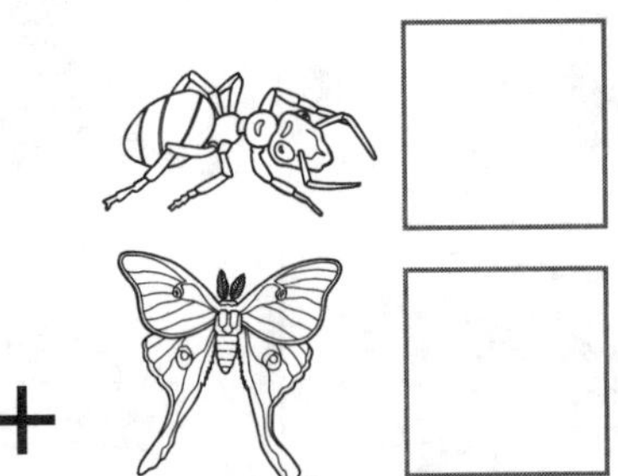

\+

9.

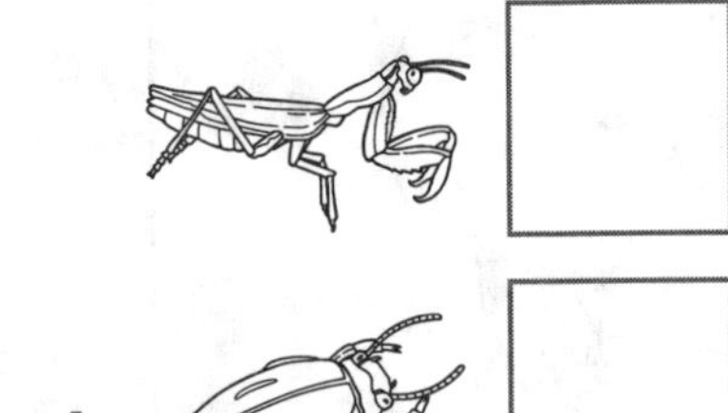

\+

Name: ______________________________

Insect Subtraction

Use the math mural to write the numbers in the squares.
Subtract the numbers.

1.

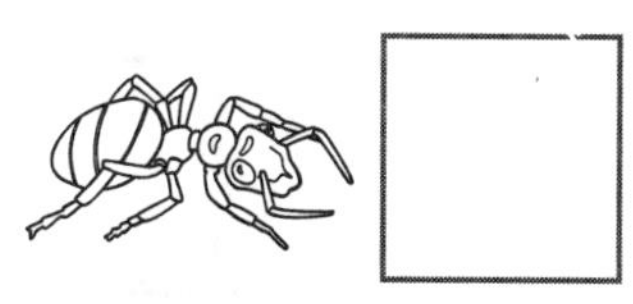

—

2.

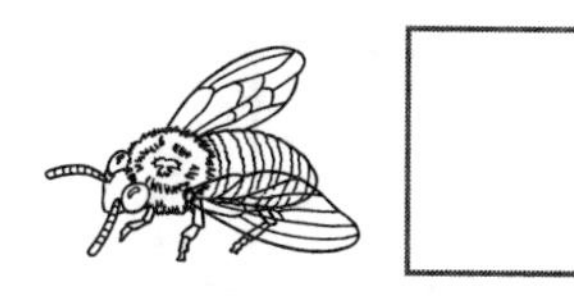

—

3.

—

4.

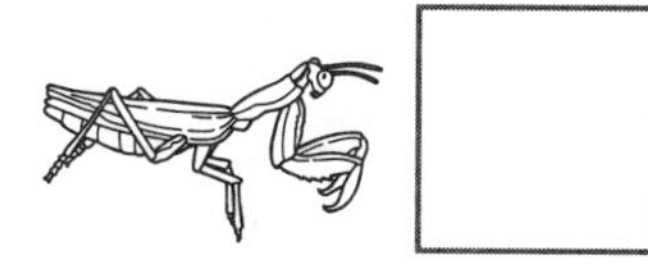

—

5.

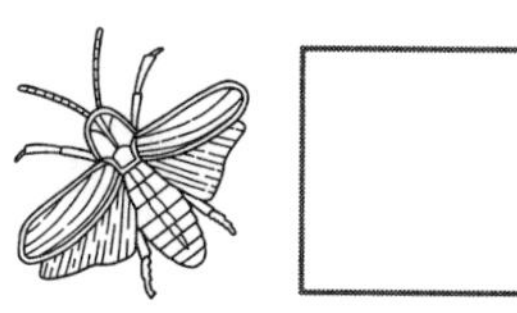

—

6.

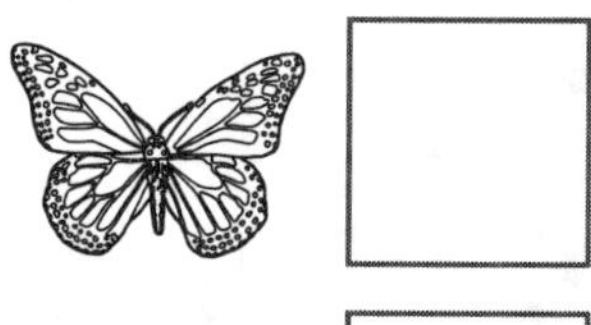

—

7.

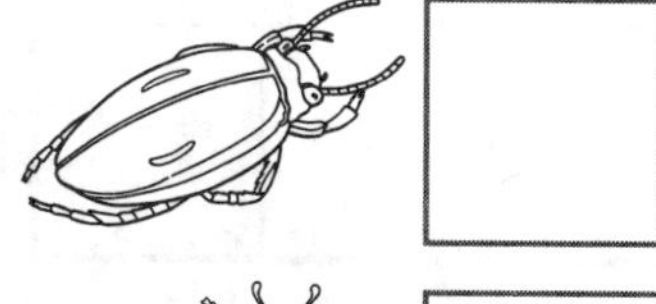

—

8.

—

9.

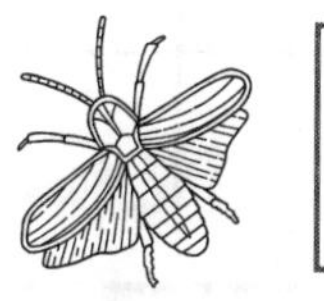

—

Name: ______________________________

Insect Graphing

Use the math mural to count the different kinds of insects.
Color the graph to show how many of each kind you count.

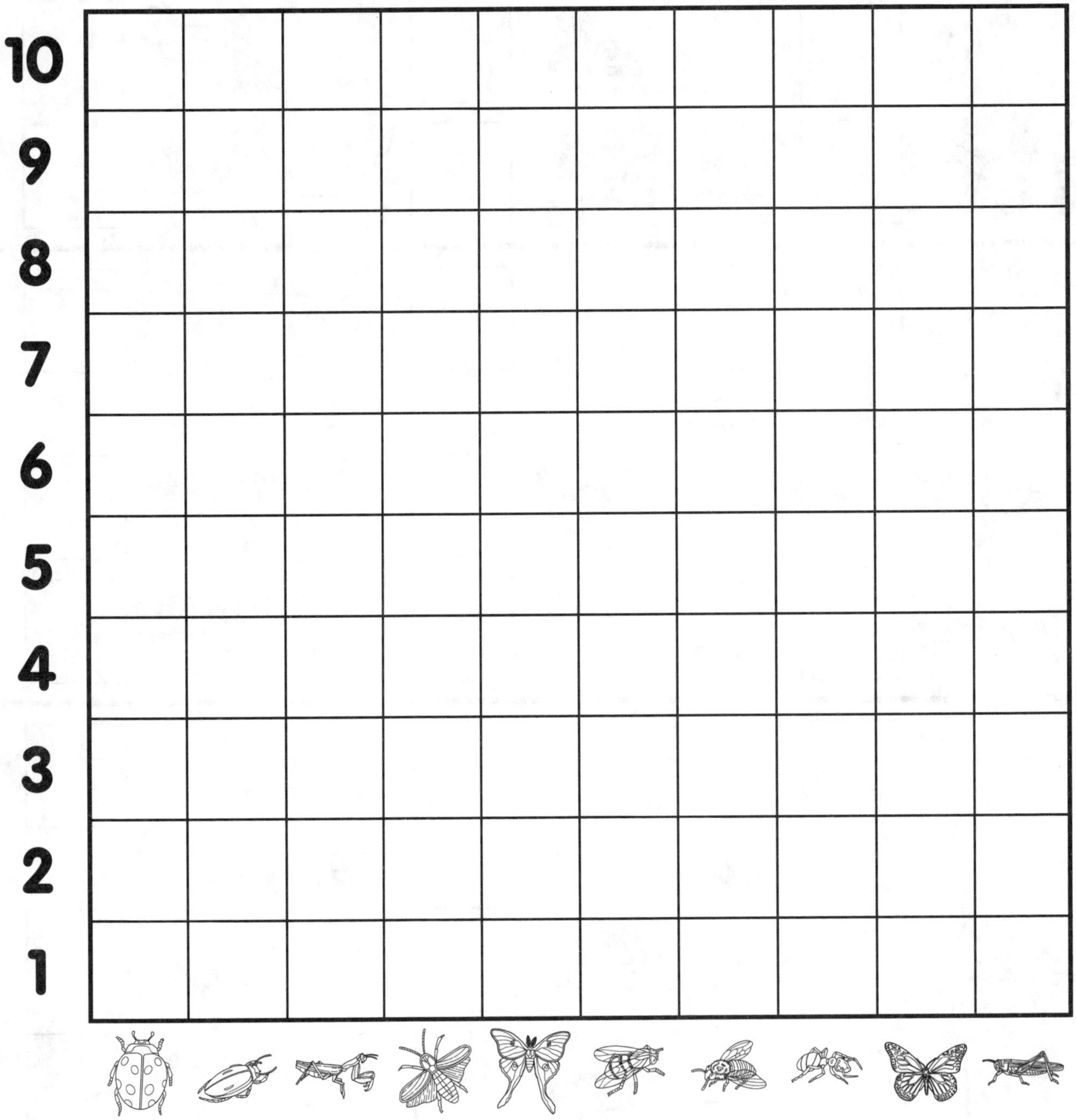

10										
9										
8										
7										
6										
5										
4										
3										
2										
1										

Name: ______________________________

Insect Questions

Use the math mural to answer the questions.

1. How many luna moths and monarch butterflies are there in all? ________

2. How many more ants are there than ladybugs? ________

3. If the fireflies, bees, and flies all fly away, how many would that be? ________

4. Each ladybug has 10 spots. How many spots are there altogether? Count by 10's or multiply. ________

5. The water bugs all have two antennae. How many antennae are there on the water bugs in all? Count by 2's. ________

6. Estimate how many flying insects are in the picture. Include flies, bees, luna moths, monarch butterflies, fireflies, and ladybugs. Then count how many are in the picture. ________

7. How long is the praying mantis from head to tail? Measure to the nearest half inch. ________

8. Measure the wing span of the firefly in centimeters. ________

Merry Math Tales

Talking About the Theme: Fairy Tales

Fairy tales are a literary genre that crosses both cultural and generational boundaries. Not only are some stories common to different groups, but the tales also connect children, parents, and grandparents in many families. This Fairy Tale math mural offers an opportunity to revisit favorite stories, to create new adventures for archetypal characters, and to practice math skills as well.

Plan to leave the mural in place for several weeks, so that you can take full advantage of this popular theme.

Materials

The materials needed to assemble this bulletin board are:

- fairy tale character patterns on pages 61-65
- border patterns on page 66
- roll of light green and roll of light blue craft paper
- yellow, brown, gray, pink, tan, green, and white construction paper
- crayons or colored markers
- scissors
- stapler

Getting Started with the Mini-Mural

On page 57 you'll find a reproducible mini-mural. This mini-mural is a good way to introduce the theme and the concept of doing math with a mural. It also provides a template for placing the characters on the large mural.

Make a copy of the mini-mural for each child. Talk about the fairy tales from which each character comes. Have the children decide who lives in each house and each castle.

Who lives in the houses? straw, stick, and brick houses (Three Little Pigs); gingerbread house (Hansel and Gretel); Three Bears' house (Bears); dwarfs' cottage (Snow White); house of Cinderella's stepmother (Cinderella).

Who lives in the castles? Sleeping Beauty, Rapunzel, The Princess and the Pea, and The Frog Prince.

By naming the houses or castles for characters not already in the mural, you increase the number of fairy tales that you can integrate into your story problems. For example:

- If each prince asked a princess to dance, how many princes would not have a partner?
- If the wolf, pigs, and bears all climbed up Rapunzel's hair for a visit, how many visitors would she have?

Children will soon understand how to create their own problems based on the characters, houses, castles, and trees. Explain that they will be creating a similar mural on the bulletin board for more math fun.

Assembling the Bulletin Board

Follow these steps to create your Fairy Tale bulletin board. You may wish to have children work in groups to prepare the different characters (steps 3-4) and border patterns (step 7) while you complete the background.

1 Using light green craft paper, cover most of the bulletin board. Cut a wavy line at the top to represent hills.

2 Add light blue craft paper at the top to represent sky.

3 Duplicate the patterns on pages 61-65. You may choose to enlarge or reduce the images depending on the size of your bulletin board. Here are some coloring suggestions:

10 trees on white paper; color trunks brown and leaves green

9 princes on white paper (4 on horseback and 5 standing)

8 houses on white paper

7 dwarfs on white paper with clothing colored green

6 princesses on white paper

5 castles on gray paper with different-colored flags

4 pigs on white paper with different-colored clothes

3 bears on brown paper

2 witches on gray paper with green faces

1 wolf on brown paper

4 Have children cut out and color the patterns. Suggest that they decorate the houses and characters to go with different fairy tales. Encourage children to add details such as a nightcap for the wolf or an apple for one of the witches.

BOARD TIP

Ask for children's help in adding details. For example, you might put one castle in the air with a beanstalk leading to it, or you might designate a princess to be Rapunzel and put her in a castle tower.

5 Staple the patterns onto the bulletin board following the mini-mural arrangement.

6 Duplicate the border patterns on yellow paper. Note that there is a different pattern for each side of the math mural.

7 Have children color the border characters as follows:

Red Riding Hood = red cape, blue skirt, red shoes

Puss in Boots = brown boots, blue clothes, red feather

troll = brown clothes and hair, green body

goats = white

8 Staple the borders along the sides of the bulletin board display.

9 Duplicate the display title. Ask a student to color it before you add it to the mural.

MERRY MATH TALES

Using the Merry Math Tales Mural

You'll find that, as with the other themes, the Fairy Tale mural is very versatile. You can use it for practicing counting, adding, subtracting, multiplying, graphing, and much more. You might begin by giving students problems such as these, then move on to having students make up their own problems. You'll also want to use the worksheets on pages 67-70.

Sample Story Problems

- If each dwarf hides behind a tree, how many trees do not have a dwarf behind them?
- Can each of the princesses live in her own castle?

Sample Pattern Problem

- What is the pattern on the top border?

Sample Estimation Problem

- Estimate the number of Little Red Riding Hoods on the border. Count to check your answer.

Using the Worksheets

Duplicate and assign the worksheets on pages 67-70. Have children work with partners to check one another's papers.

Adding with Fairy Tale Friends

Remind students to use the math mural to determine the number for each picture. For example, for the first problem they would write 7 (dwarfs) and 10 (trees). Students should then complete the addition. Conclude by asking children how to check their work.

Subtracting with Fairy Tale Friends

Have children follow the same procedure, using the math mural, to determine the numbers for each problem.

Graphing with Fairy Tale Friends

Children can use this page to make a graph showing how many of each pattern are on the math mural. Have students make up questions based on their graphs. For example:

- Are there more houses or castles?
- How many animals are there in all?

Fairy Tale Story Problems

Children can create and record their own problems on this page. Set aside time for students to share their story problems with the class.

Cross-Curricular Activities

Language Arts

- Set up a fairy tale reading center which includes books and tapes. Try to include fairy tales from other countries and parodies of original fairy tales. You might have children read similar fairy tales within the same week. For example, the class might concentrate on tales involving "big and little." Examples include *Tom Thumb* and *Jack and the Beanstalk*. Other categories might be "royalty" or tales with the number three.

- Review these elements of a fairy tale as defined by Regie Routman in her book *Invitations*:

  1. Happens in the past— the period not defined
  2. Usually has a happy ending
  3. May involve the supernatural
  4. Often has a clear conflict between good and evil
  5. Often begins with "Once upon a time"
  6. Often includes a task, which if completed, brings a reward
  7. Has a plot and problem
  8. Often includes a magic object or person to help the main character
  9. Often has a brave hero who rescues a helpless maiden
  10. Usually has to do with royalty

- Make a class ABC Fairy Tale book. Have each child be responsible for a page. For example, the W page might say: *Once wise wizards and wacky witches wandered down a windy, winding walk to a warm welcome at a weird castle with wonderful waffles.* Once children have illustrated their alliterative sentences, compile them into a book and place it in your reading center.

Drama

- Have children dramatize math problems that relate to the bulletin board characters. Children might also act out their own original fairy tales.

Social Studies

- Children will enjoy learning about real castles, knights, kings, queens, lords, ladies, coats of armor, and other fairy tale elements that are related to medieval times.

Literature Links

- *The Korean Cinderella* and *The Egyptian Cinderella* by Shirley Climo
- *The Frog Prince* and *The Three Bears* by Paul Galdone
- *Yeh-Shen* by Ai-Ling Louie
- *The True Story of the Three Little Pigs* by Jon Scieszka
- *Lon Po Po* by Ed Young
- *Rumplestiltskin* by Paul O. Zelinsky

Merry Math Tales: Reproducible Page

Use these letter patterns to name your math board. With the help of a Xerox copier you can enlarge each letter even more!

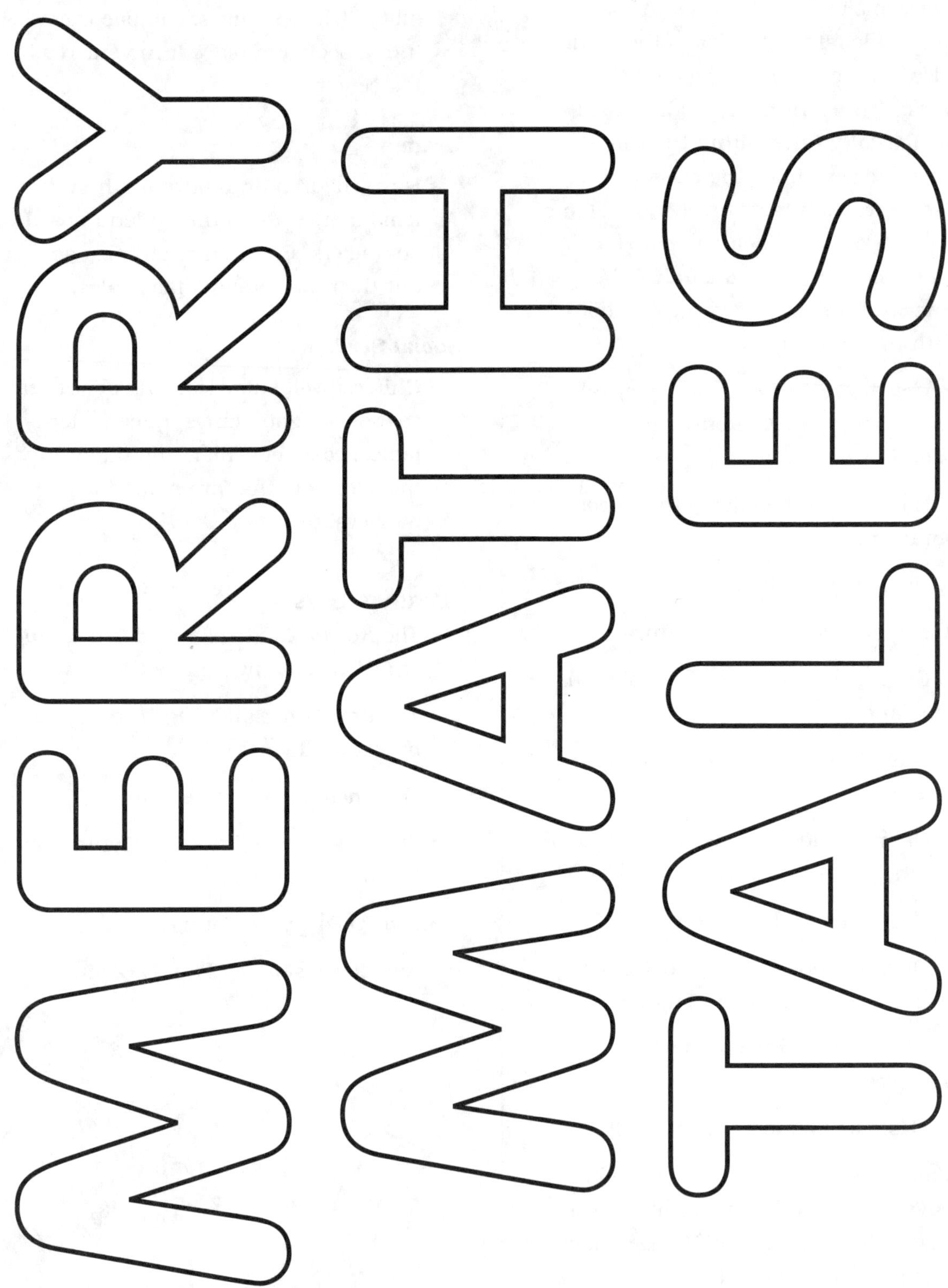

Merry Math Tales: Reproducible Page

Copy on brown paper. The numbers in parentheses suggest how many you will need of each pattern.

Merry Math Tales: Reproducible Page

Copy on gray paper. The numbers in parentheses suggest how many you will need of each pattern.

Merry Math Tales: Reproducible Page

Copy on white paper. The numbers in parentheses suggest how many you will need of each pattern. Have children color the patterns as suggested on page 55.

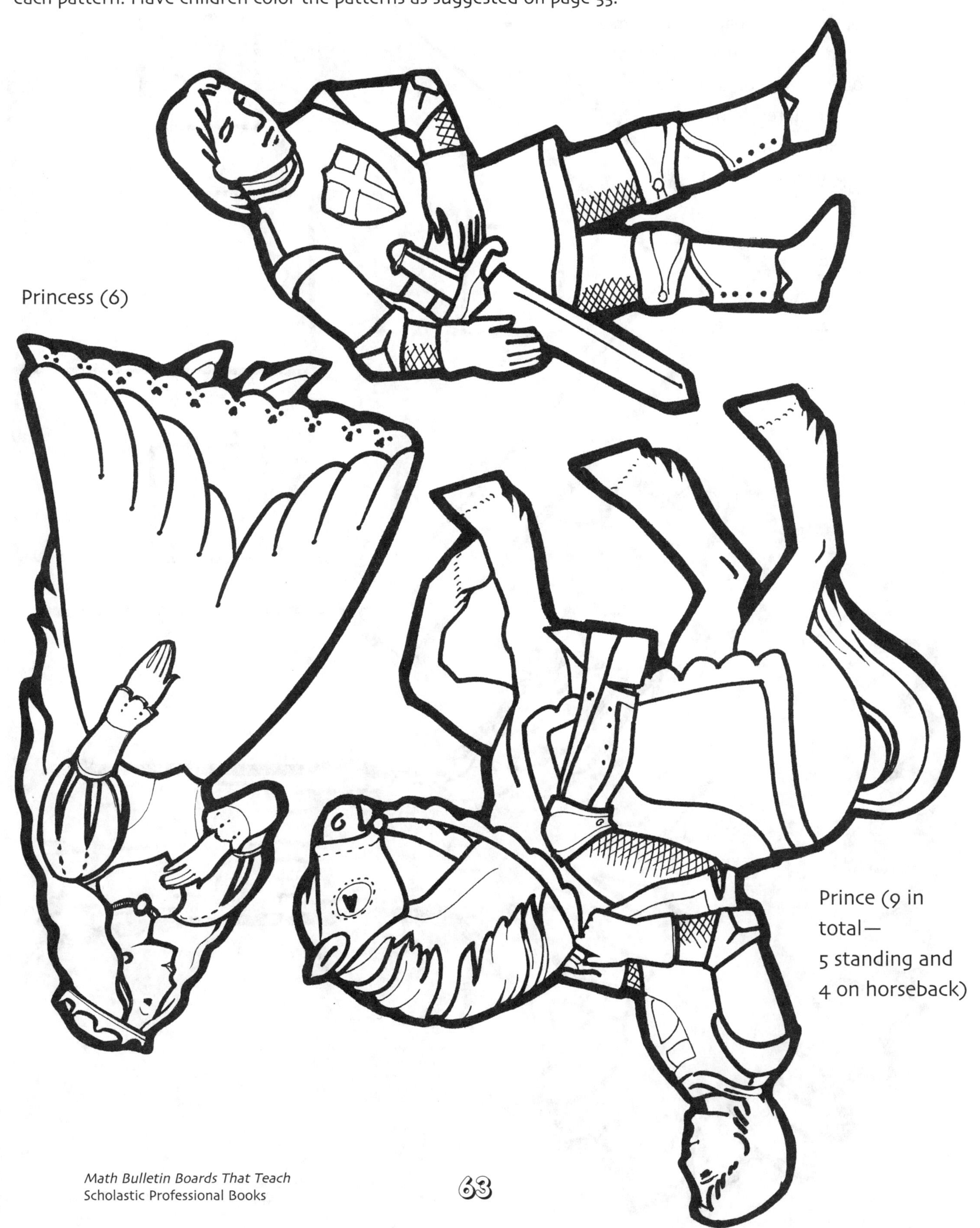

Princess (6)

Prince (9 in total—
5 standing and
4 on horseback)

Merry Math Tales: Reproducible Page

Copy on white paper. The numbers in parentheses suggest how many you will need of each pattern. Have children color the patterns as suggested on page 55.

Merry Math Tales: Reproducible Page

Copy on white paper. The numbers in parentheses suggest how many you will need of each pattern. Have children color the patterns as suggested on page 55.

Dwarf (7)

Pig (four in total—1 mother, 3 babies)

Merry Math Tales: Reproducible Page Copy the border patterns on yellow paper. Have children color them as suggested on page 56.

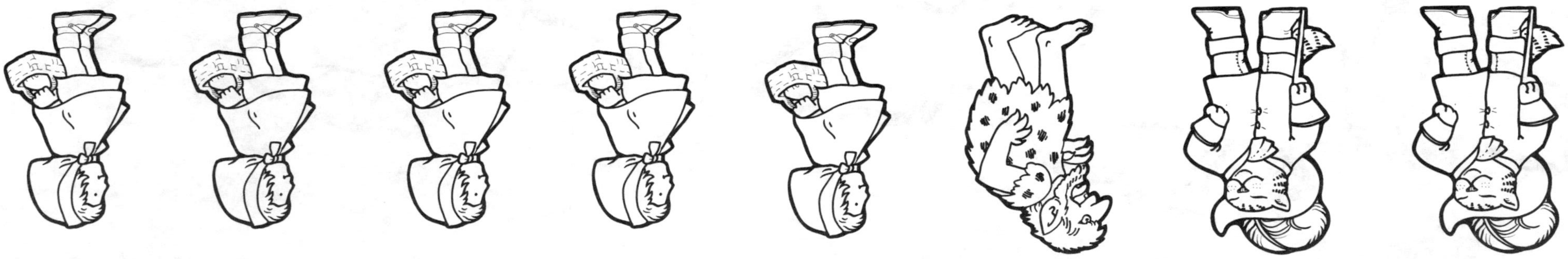

Top Border

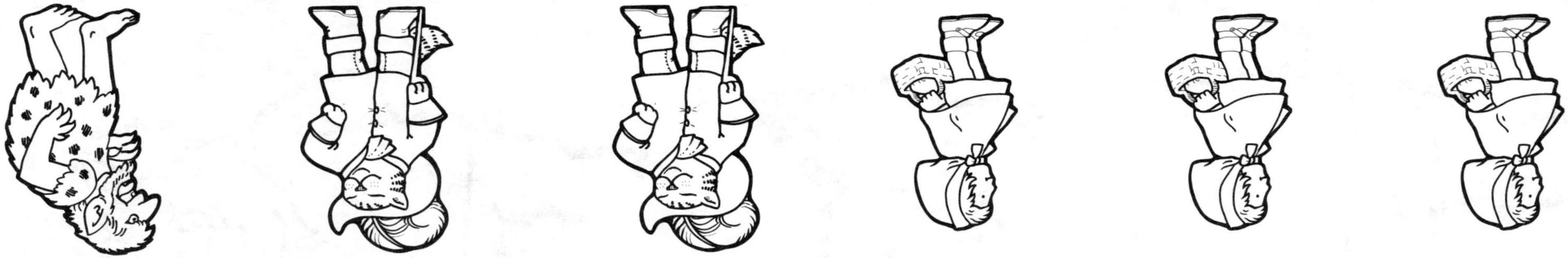

Bottom Border

Right Border

Left Border

Name: ______________________________

Adding with Fairy Tale Friends

Use the math mural to write the numbers in the squares.
Add the numbers.

1.

+

2.

+

3.

+

4.

+

5.

+

6.

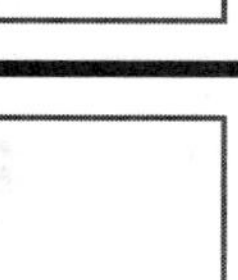

+

7.

+

8.

+

9.

+

Name: ______________________________

Subtracting with Fairy Tale Friends

Use the math mural to write the numbers in the squares.
Subtract the numbers.

1.

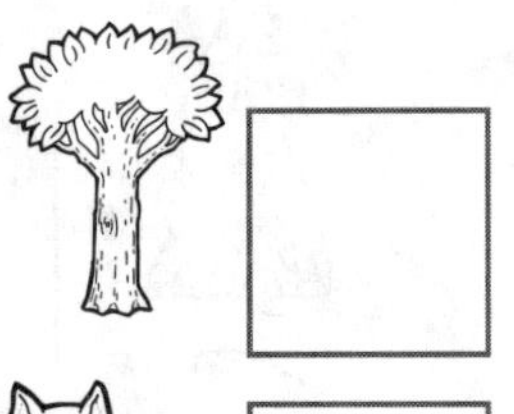

−

2.

−

3.

−

4.

−

5.

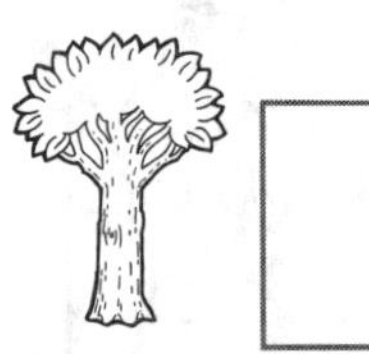

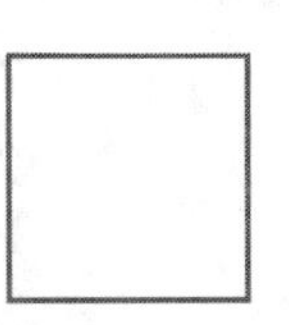

−

6.

−

7.

−

8.

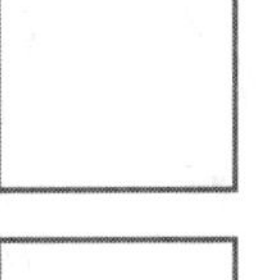

−

9.

−

Name: ______________________________

Graphing with Fairy Tale Friends

Use the math mural to count the different kinds of fairy tale patterns. Color the graph to show how many of each kind you count.

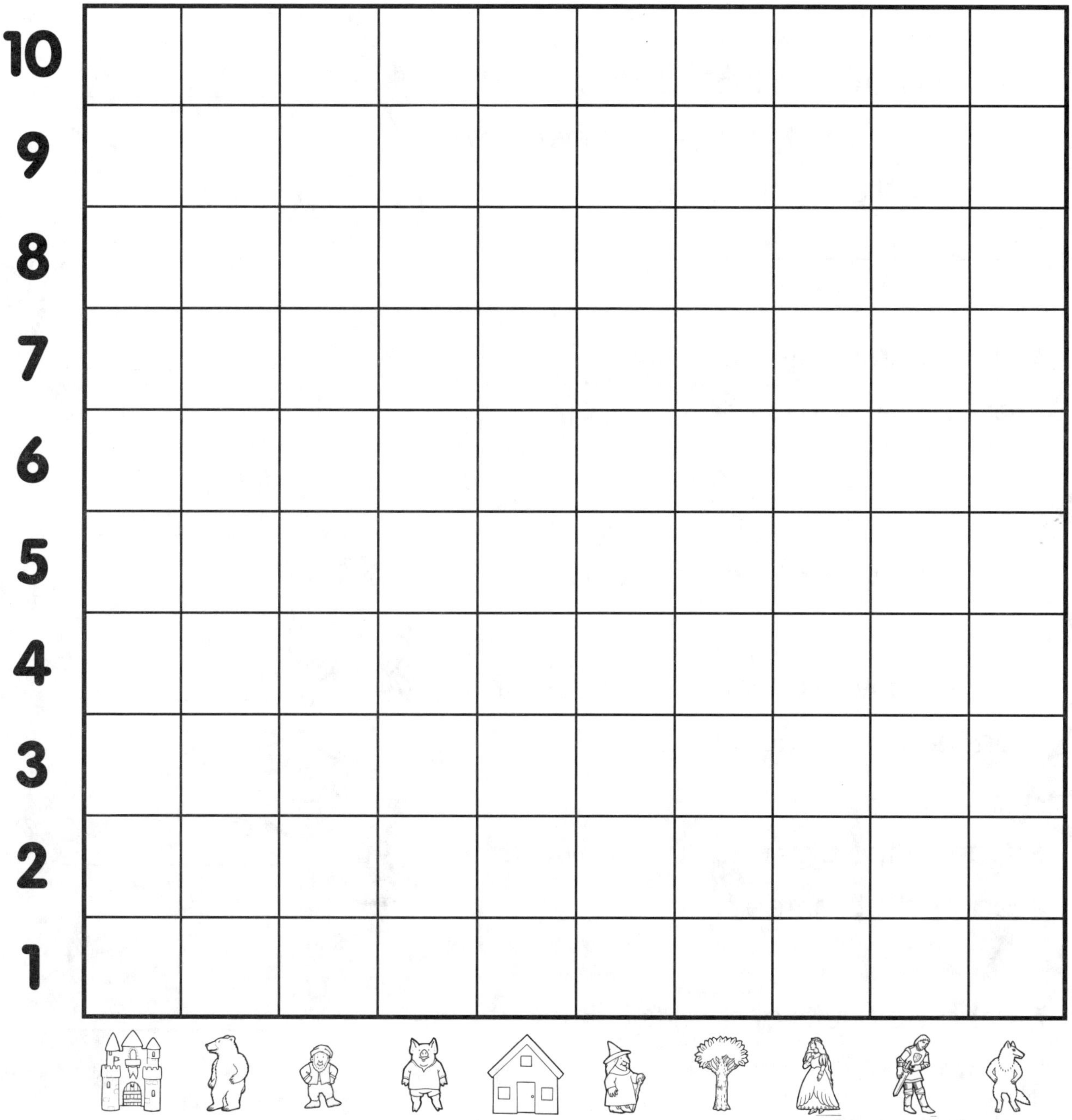

10										
9										
8										
7										
6										
5										
4										
3										
2										
1										

Name: ____________________

Fairy Tale Story Problems

Use the math mural to solve the problems.

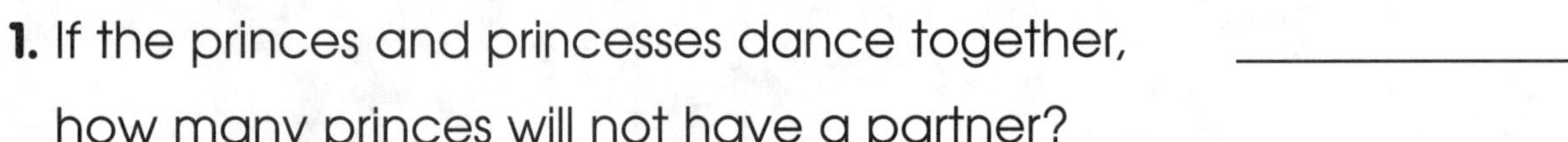

1. If the princes and princesses dance together, how many princes will not have a partner? ____________

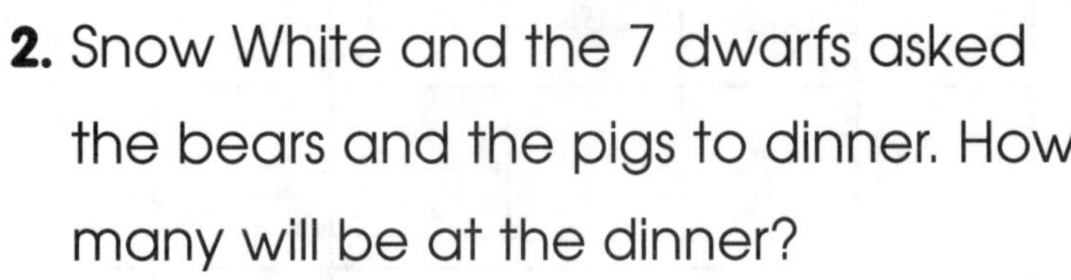

2. Snow White and the 7 dwarfs asked the bears and the pigs to dinner. How many will be at the dinner? ____________

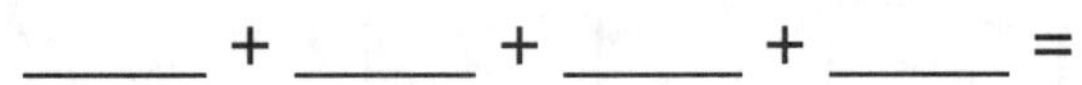

_____ + _____ + _____ + _____ =

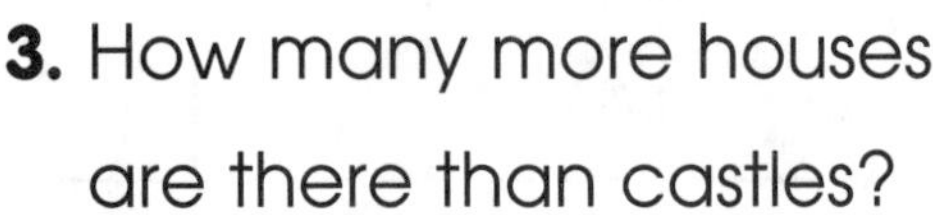

3. How many more houses are there than castles? ____________

4. How far is it (in inches) from the wolf to the third pig's brick house? ____________

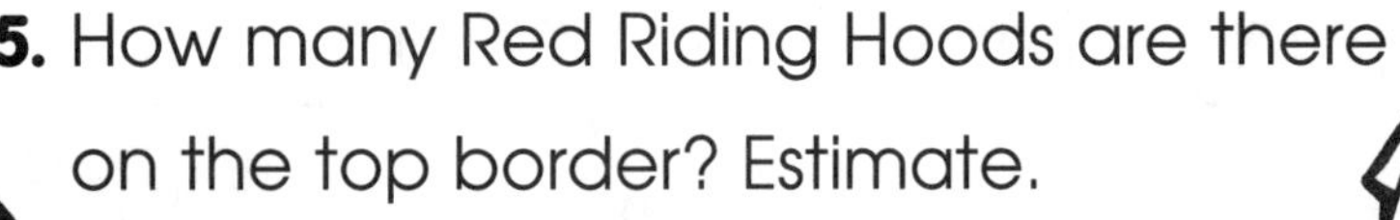

5. How many Red Riding Hoods are there on the top border? Estimate. ____________

6. Can all the pigs and all the dwarfs each climb a tree? ____________

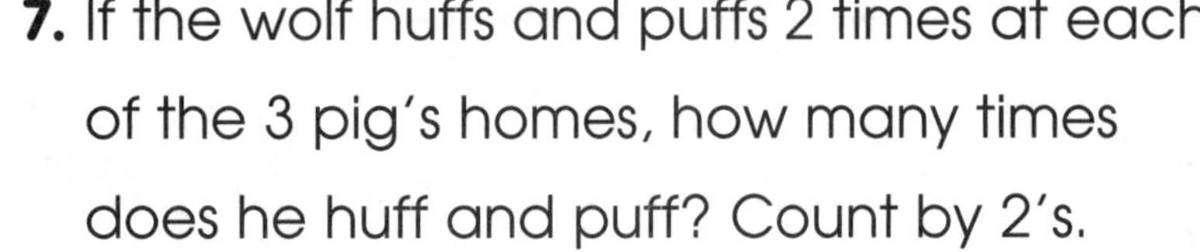

7. If the wolf huffs and puffs 2 times at each of the 3 pig's homes, how many times does he huff and puff? Count by 2's. ____________

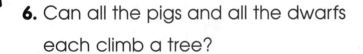

Dinomathic Park

Talking About the Theme: Dinosaurs

Dinosaurs are an ever-popular topic of interest for children. Many youngsters can pronounce and read the longest dinosaur names with greater ease than shorter, grade-level words. When you introduce Dinomathic Park, you're saying to the class, "This is no ordinary way of doing math. This is going to be fun!"

Once the Dinomathic Park mural is assembled, it will become the focal point of not only your math lessons, but other dinosaur studies as well. As a result, you'll want to leave it up for several weeks at least.

Materials

As you prepare to dig into this theme, you'll need to collect materials for assembling the math mural. You'll need:

- dinosaur patterns on pages 78-82
- border patterns on page 83
- roll of green or tan craft paper
- light blue construction paper
- red and yellow tissue paper
- crayons and markers
- scissors
- stapler

Getting Started with the Mini-Mural

On page 73 you'll find a mini-mural of Dinomathic Park. Make a copy for each child. This serves as a wonderful introduction to the math mural concept and provides a template to follow in placing the dinosaurs on the bulletin board. The mini-mural also offers an opportunity to introduce each type of dinosaur and to review the names.

An informal math lesson based on the mini-mural might include questions such as:

- How many more stegosauruses are there than triceratops?
- The trachodons are running in two equal groups. How many are there in each group?

Children will enjoy making up story problems about the dinosaurs and will be enthusiastic about creating a large bulletin board display like the mini-mural.

Assembling the Math Mural

Follow these steps to complete your Dinomathic Park math mural. You may wish to have children work in groups to prepare the dinosaurs (steps 6 and 9) while you focus on the rest of the display.

1 Cover the bulletin board with tan or light green craft paper.

2 Cut a strip of light blue paper (wavy on one side and straight on the other). Add it to the board to create a sky.

3 Cut out several ponds in light blue paper. Attach them to the board.

4 Cut some tan paper to make volcanoes. Staple these on the board and add red and yellow tissue to make hot lava.

5 Duplicate the dinosaur patterns on pages 78-83. You may choose to enlarge or reduce the images depending on the size of your bulletin board. I suggest using the following amounts so that you can coordinate the mural with the math worksheets on pages 84-89. Tell children that the real color of dinosaurs is unknown, so you have chosen some colors for them.

10 coelophysis in gray

9 stegosaurus in yellow

8 ankylosaurus in orange

7 triceratops in brown

6 trachodon in blue

5 tyrannosaurus rex in green

4 acrocanthosaurus in tan

3 corythosaurus in purple

2 brachiosaurus in gray

1 elasmosaurus in red

6 Have students cut out the dinosaurs. Children might want to color the teeth or horns; however, each type of dinosaur should be colored the same way for easy identification. As an alternative, you can duplicate the patterns on colored construction paper.

7 Staple the dinosaurs onto the bulletin board either duplicating the mini-mural or in an arrangement that children suggest.

8 Duplicate the four border patterns. Note that there is a different pattern for each side of the bulletin board. Light yellow is a good background color for this border.

9 Instruct students to color the border dinosaurs as follows:

spinosaurus = green

velociraptor = gray

pteranodon = brown

Staple the borders along the bulletin board sides.

10 Duplicate the display title on page 77. Ask a volunteer to color the letters before you add it to the mural. You might want to duplicate it in light green construction paper.

DINOMATHIC PARK

Using the Dinomathic Park Mural

You can use your dinosaur math mural in a variety of ways. You might begin by giving children problems such as the ones shown here. Then encourage students to make up their own problems. You'll also want to assign the reproducible worksheets on pages 84-89.

Sample Story Problems

- How many more stegosauruses are there than acrocanthosauruses?
- If the elasmosaurus visits the trachodons, how many dinosaurs will be in the group?

Sample Pattern Problems

- Describe the pattern on the top of the mural. How many times does this pattern repeat itself?
- Give each dinosaur in the pattern on the right side of the mural a number. What is the number pattern for this border?

Sample Estimation Problems

- Estimate how many of each kind of dinosaur there are on the left border. Count to check.
- Estimate how many dinosaurs there are in the main part of the mural. Count to check.

Measuring

Before introducing a measuring activity, mark one of each kind of dinosaur with two black dots to indicate the points children should measure. In some cases you can have your students measure height, and in others, length. Have them measure in inches on one day and in centimeters on another. You can also have students measure distances between various dinosaurs.

Multiplication

To work with multiplication concepts, place the dinosaurs on the mural in groups. For example, you might show 3 groups of 3 stegosauruses, 4 groups of 2 ankylosauruses, 2 groups of 3 trachodons, and 2 groups of 2 acrocanthosauruses. You can also use the border patterns for multiplication because they are arranged in groups of 2, 3, 4, and 5. Ask children to write both an addition problem and a multiplication problem for each set of dinosaurs.

Division

Once children can visualize dinosaurs in groups for multiplication, they can understand how the groups are divided. For example, they can see that the 9 stegosauruses are divided into 3 groups of 3 each.

Counting by 2's, 5's, and 10's

Have children practice counting skills based on stories about the dinosaurs. For example: If each triceratops eats 5 plants today, how many plants will they eat in all?

Using the Worksheets

To focus students on various skills, provide them with copies of the reproducible worksheets. You might wish to have children work with partners to check one another's work.

Dinomathic Park Addition

Have students write number problems to match the pictures on the bulletin board. For the first problem, they would write 1 elasmosaurus and 7 triceratops. Students should then complete the addition and show how they can check their work.

Dinomathic Park Addition of 3 Numbers

Children follow the same procedure, but on this page they add three numbers.

Dinomathic Park Subtraction

For this page, children again use the bulletin board to determine the number of dinosaurs for each problem.

Dinomathic Park Graphing

Students can use this page to make a graph showing how many of each kind of dinosaur are on the bulletin board. Once the graphs are completed, have children make up questions about them. Model examples such as:

- How many brachiosauruses are there?
- Are there as many corythosauruses as trachodons?
- How does the graph help organize the data about the dinosaurs?

My Own Questions

On this page students create their own word problems. Explain that they can use any dinosaur from the bulletin board. Point out that item 6 involves measuring. Be sure to invite children to challenge the class with their questions.

Dinomathic Park Money

After children complete this page, encourage them to count aloud and point to the coins they would use for each purpose. You might also extend the activity by asking questions such as:

- If a stegosaurus costs 60 cents, would you have enough money to buy it?
- If a trachodon costs 45 cents, could you buy more than one?

Cross-Curricular Activities

Language Arts

- Students will enjoy reading both fiction and nonfiction books about dinosaurs. This is a good unit to use in teaching reference skills since many nonfiction books will have a table of contents and an index. Model how to use these reference tools as students expand their knowledge about dinosaurs.
- Invite children to use their information about dinosaurs to write a riddle about one. Can the rest of the class guess the answer?
- Make a list of new vocabulary words. In addition to the names of the dinosaurs you study, include words

such as *Mesozoic*, *Triassic*, *Jurassic*, *Cretaceous*, and *era*.

Science

- Teach a lesson on the differences between bird-hipped and lizard-hipped dinosaurs.
- Explore how fossils are formed.
- Make a chart comparing meat-eating and plant-eating dinosaurs.

Social Studies

- Introduce the terms *archeologist* and *paleontologist*. Then make a mini-dig site using a box of sand and the bones from a model dinosaur. Have students "discover" five or six bones each day and write about their findings in a paleontologist journal. Invite students to bring in their own plastic and stuffed dinosaurs to put in a classroom Dinosaur Museum.
- Have children identify on a map the places where dinosaur fossils have been found.
- Visit a local museum that has a dinosaur display.

Literature Links

- *Dinosaur Bones* and *My Visit to the Dinosaurs* by Aliki
- *Patrick's Dinosaurs* and *Big Old Bones* by Carol Carrick
- *Danny and the Dinosaur* by Syd Hoff
- *Dinosaur Bob* by William Joyce
- *Dinosaur Time* by Peggy Parish

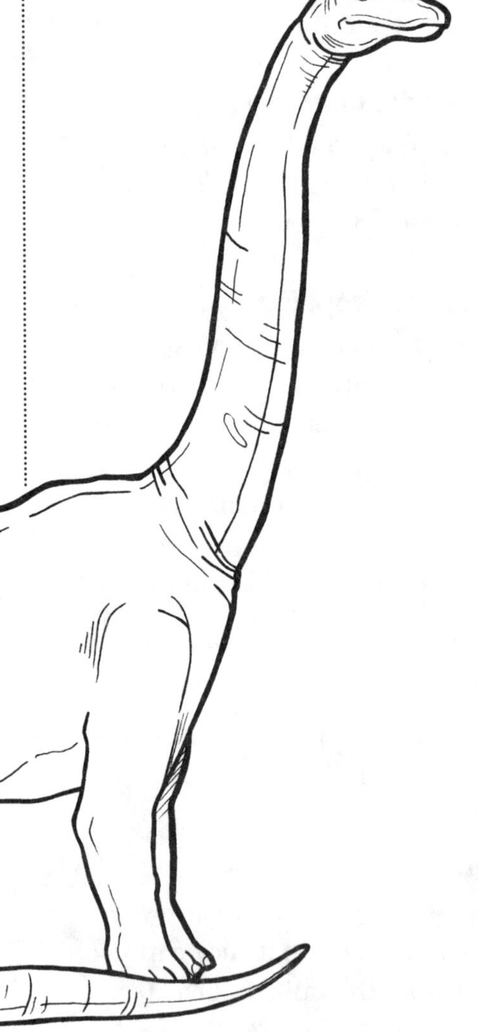

Dinomathic Park: Reproducible Page

Use these letter patterns to name your math board. With the help of a Xerox copier you can enlarge each letter even more!

Dinomathic Park: Reproducible Page

Copy on white paper. The numbers in parentheses suggest how many you will need of each pattern. Have children color the dinosaurs as suggested or copy on colored paper.

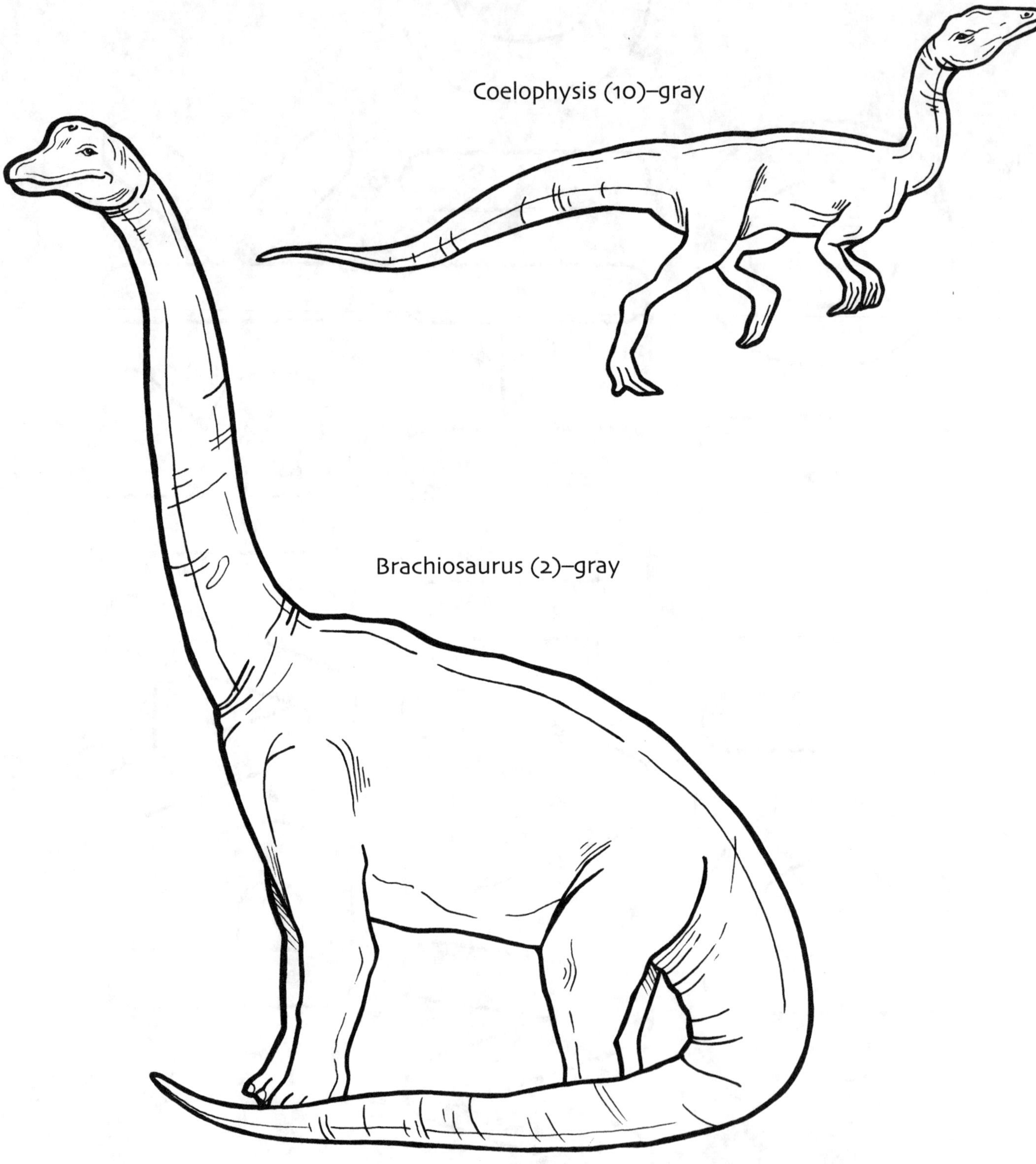

Dinomathic Park: Reproducible Page

Copy on white paper. The numbers in parentheses suggest how many you will need of each pattern. Have children color the dinosaurs as suggested or copy on colored paper.

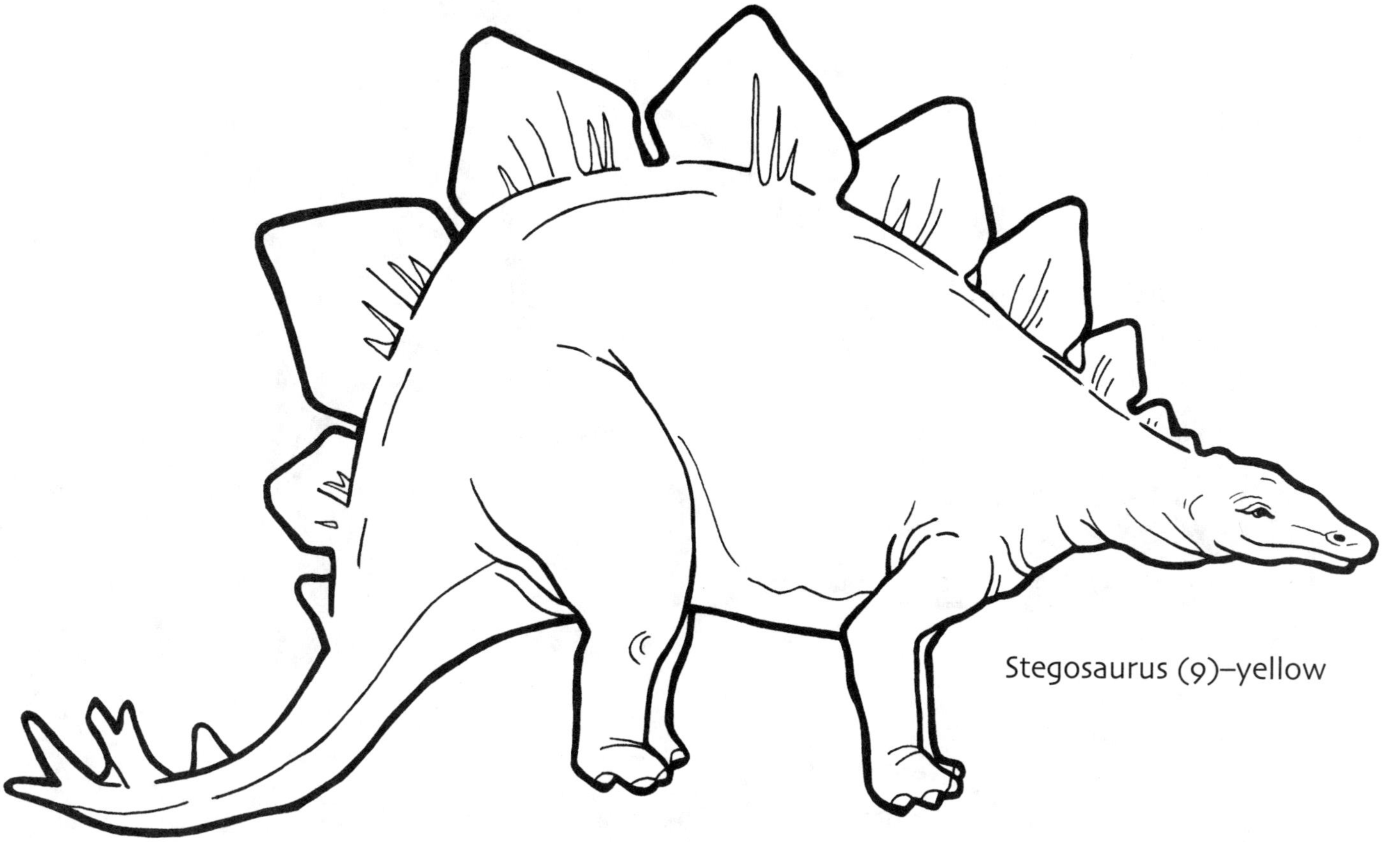

Stegosaurus (9)–yellow

Ankylosaurus (8)–orange

Dinomathic Park: Reproducible Page

Copy on white paper. The numbers in parentheses suggest how many you will need of each pattern. Have children color the dinosaurs as suggested or copy on colored paper.

Dinomathic Park: Reproducible Page

Copy on white paper. The numbers in parentheses suggest how many you will need of each pattern. Have children color the dinosaurs as suggested or copy on colored paper.

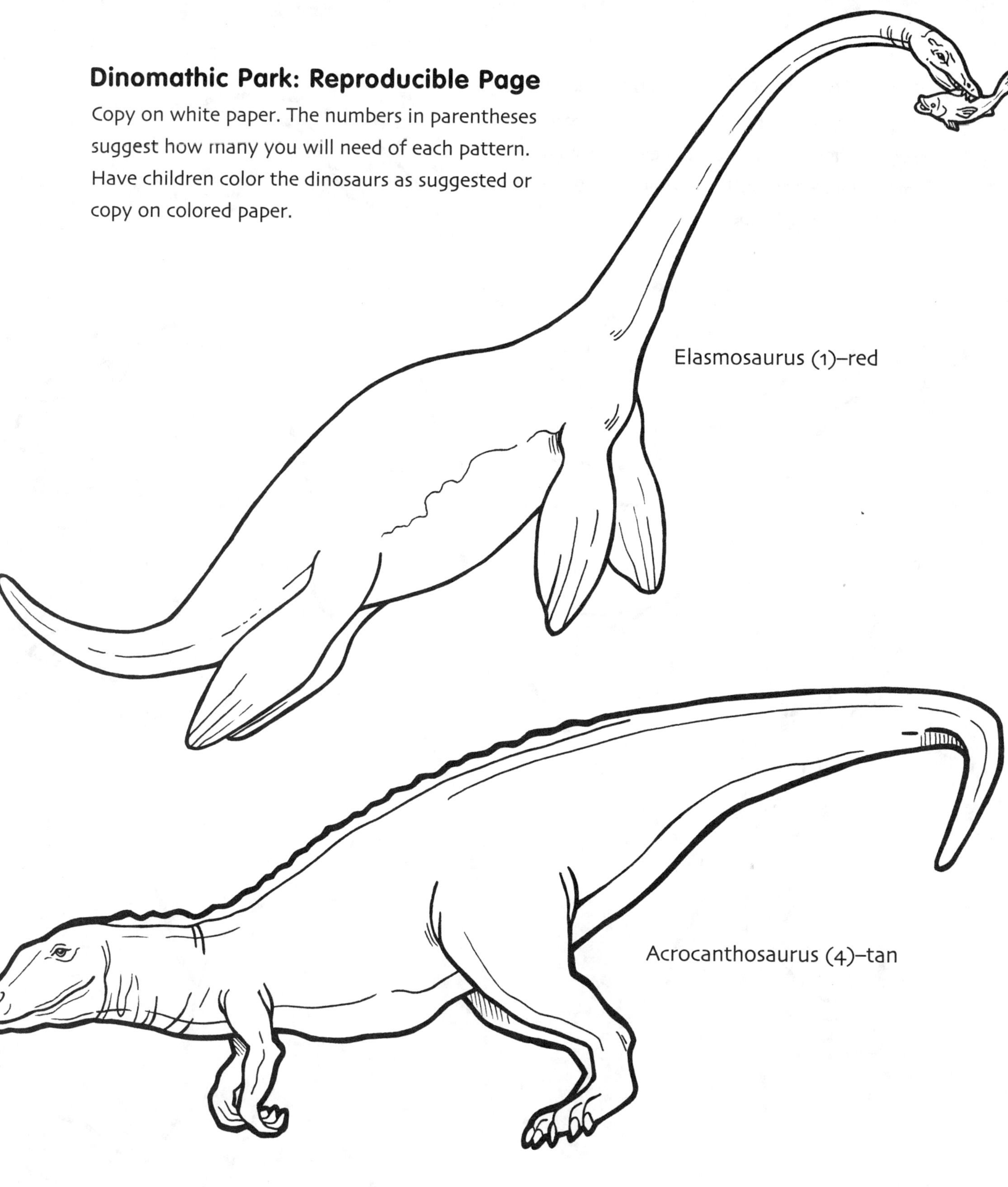

Dinomathic Park: Reproducible Page

Copy on white paper. The numbers in parentheses suggest how many you will need of each pattern. Have children color the dinosaurs as suggested or copy on colored paper.

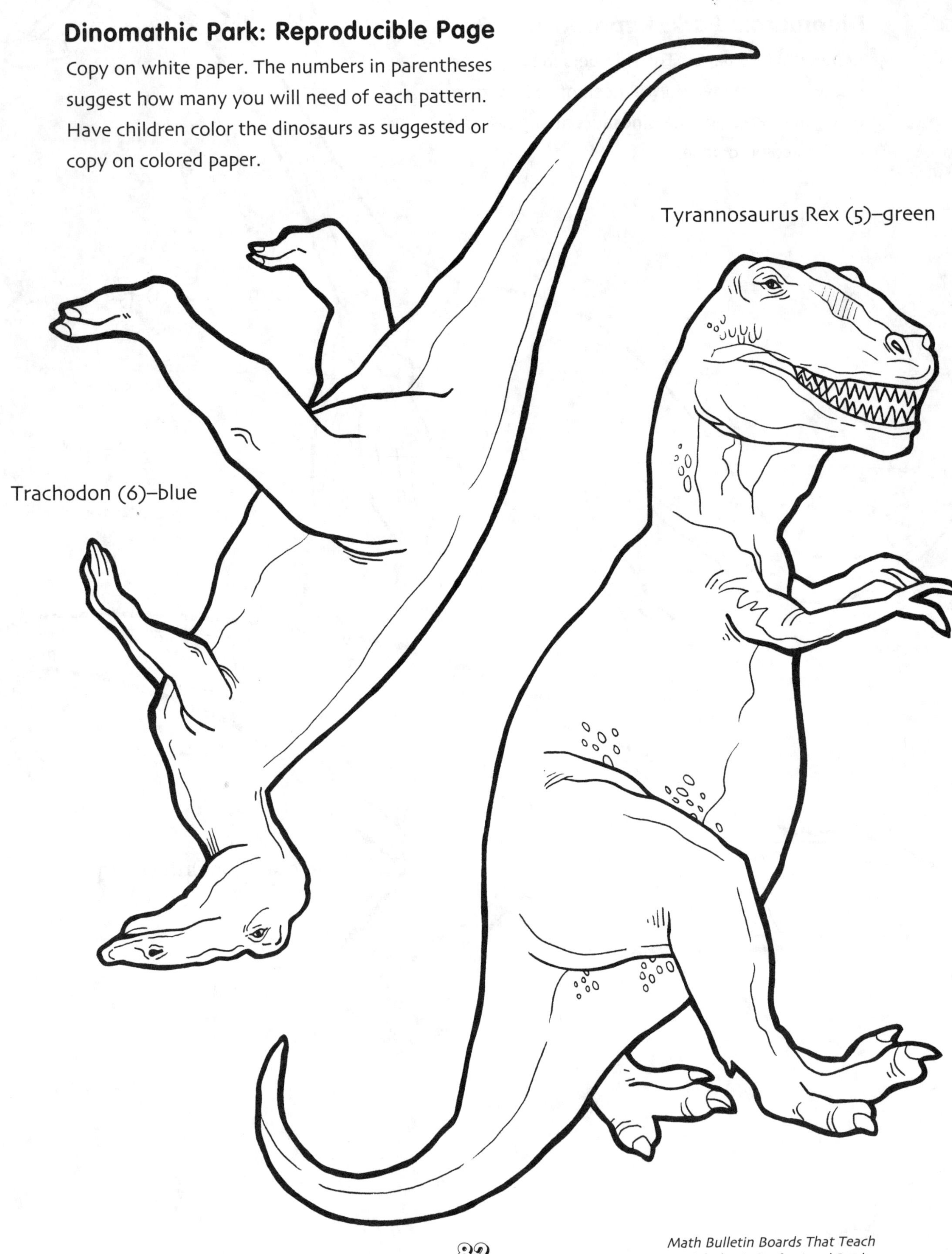

Dinomathic Park: Reproducible Page Copy the border patterns on white paper. Have children color them as suggested on page 72.

Top Border

Bottom Border

Right Border

Left Border

Name: ______________________________

Dinomathic Park Addition

Use the math mural to write the numbers in the squares.

Add the numbers.

1.

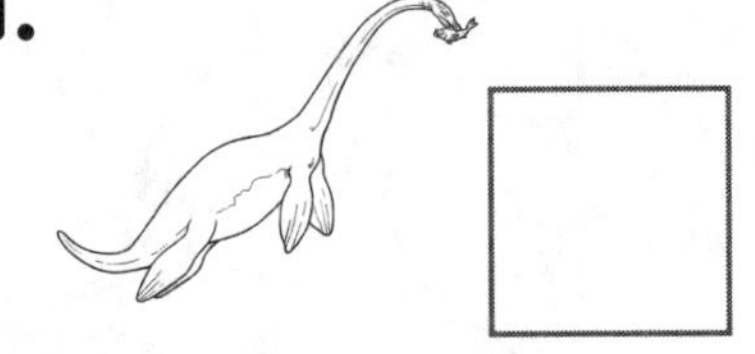

\+ 

2.

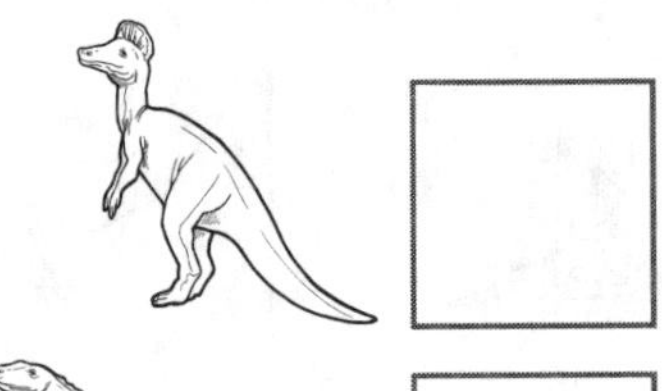

\+

3.

\+

4.

\+

5.

\+ 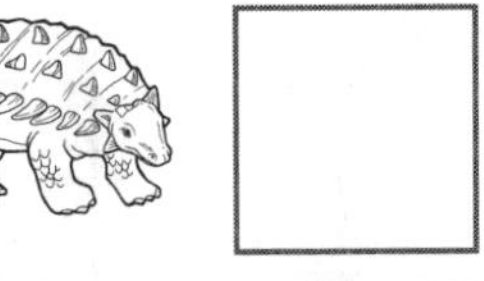

6.

\+ 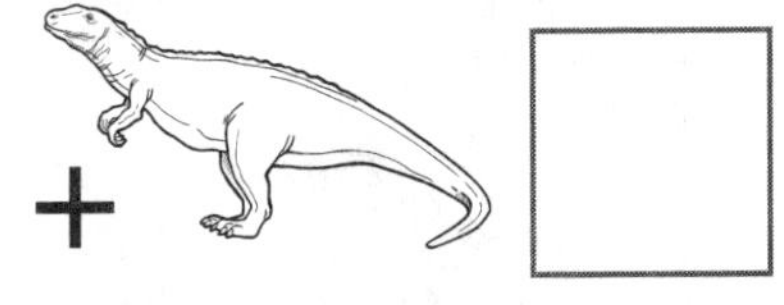

7.

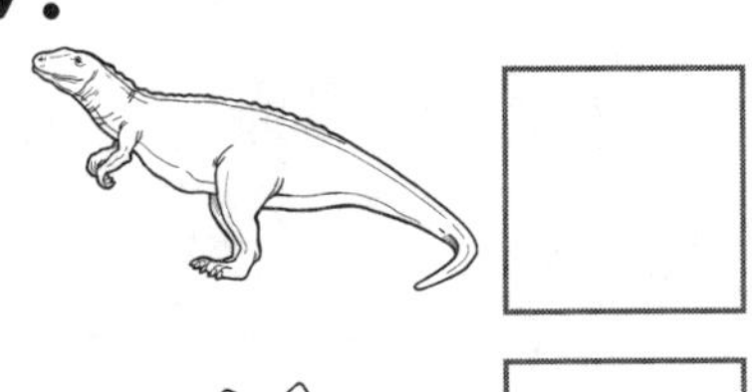

\+ 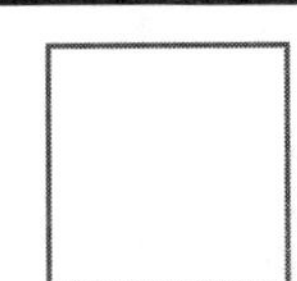

8.

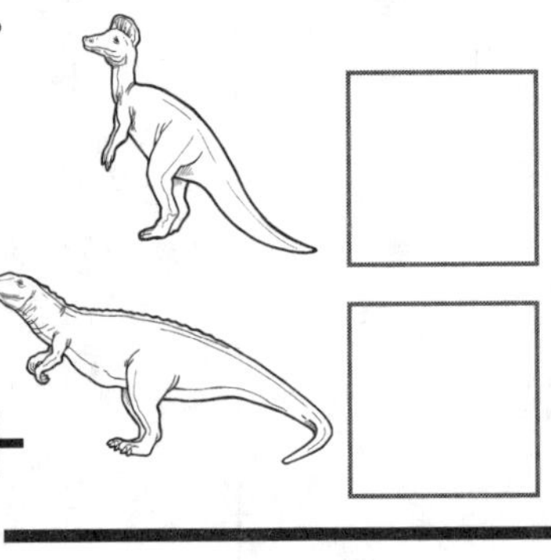

\+

9.

\+

Name: ______________________________

Dinomathic Park Addition of 3 Numbers

Use the math mural to write the numbers in the squares.
Add the numbers.

1.

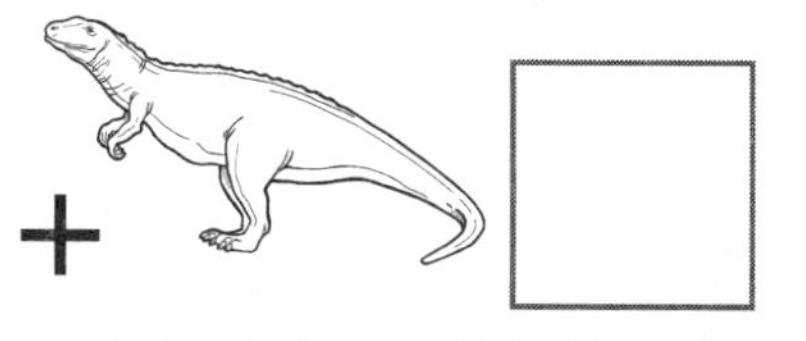

+

2.

+

3.

+

4.

+

5.

+

6.

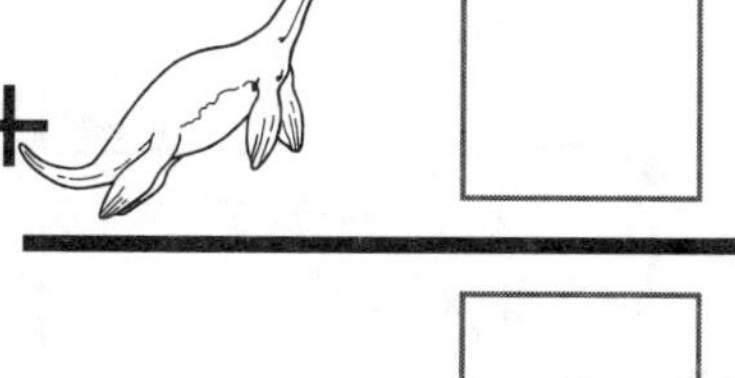

+

Name: ______________________________

Dinomathic Park Subtraction

Use the math mural to write the numbers in the squares.
Subtract the numbers.

1.

−

2.

−

3.

−

4.

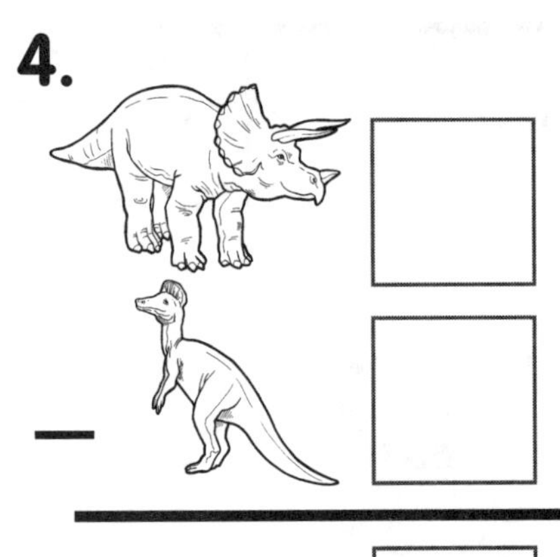

−

5.

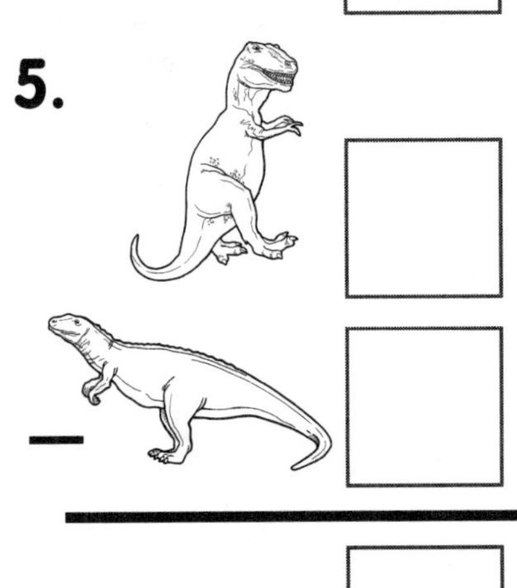

−

6.

−

7.

−

8.

−

9.

−

Name: ______________________________

Dinomathic Park Graphing

Use the math mural to count the different dinosaurs.
Color the graph to show how many of each picture you count.

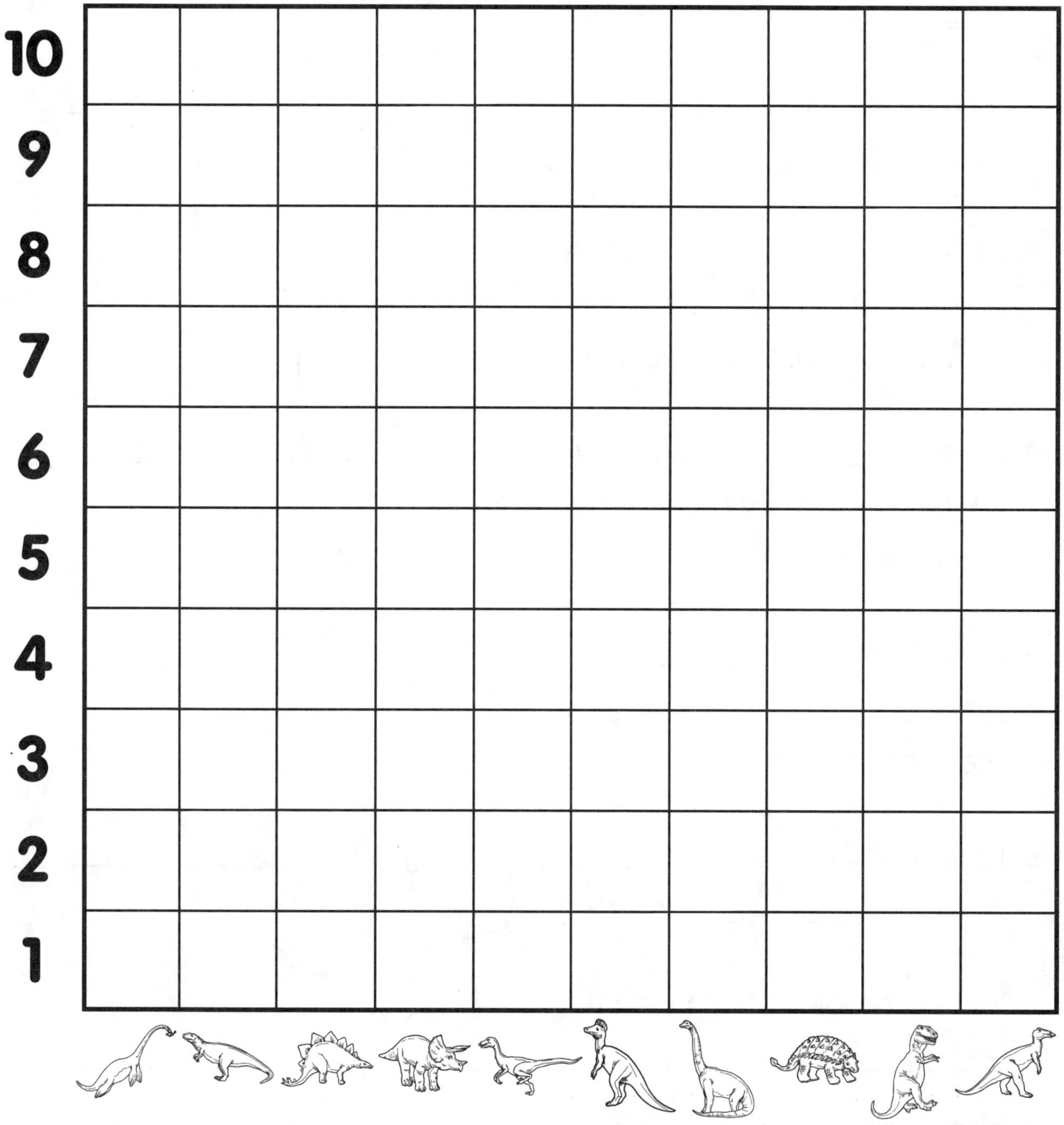

10										
9										
8										
7										
6										
5										
4										
3										
2										
1										

Name: ____________________

My Own Questions

Use the math mural to solve the problems.

1. How many ____________ and ____________ are there in all? ____________

2. How many more ________ are there than ____________? ____________

3. Each ____________ eats two plants a day. How many plants will they eat all together today? ____________

4. All of the ________ eat 5 plants a day. How many plants will they eat in all today? ____________

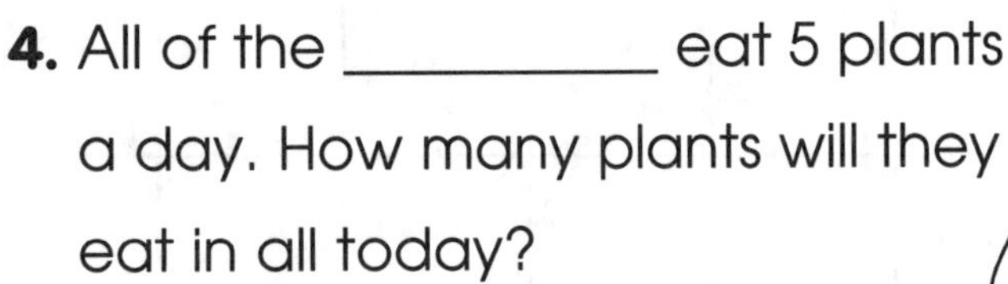

5. How many ________ and ________ and ____________ are there in all? ____________

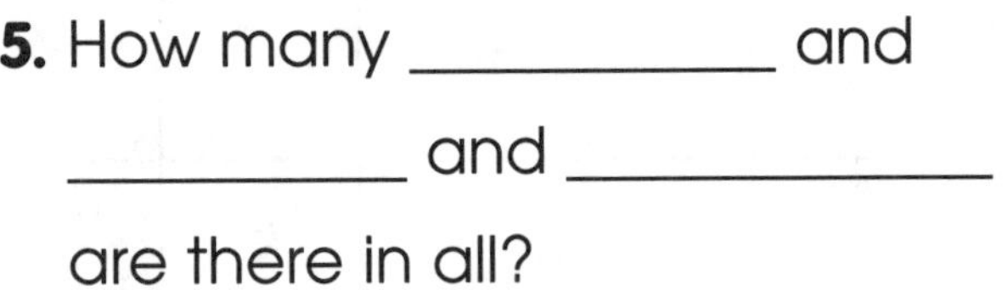

6. How much bigger is the ________ than the ________? ____________

7. Write a problem of your own.

____

____

____

Name: ______________________________

Dinomathic Park Money

Circle the money you need to pay for each dinosaur.

---

1. 36¢

---

2. 51¢

---

3. 82¢

---

4. 67¢

---

5. $1.20

Reproducible Mini-Characters

Copy these mini-characters onto the blank reproducible worksheets on pages 91-95 to create your own worksheets. You can also have students make up pages for their classmates to do.

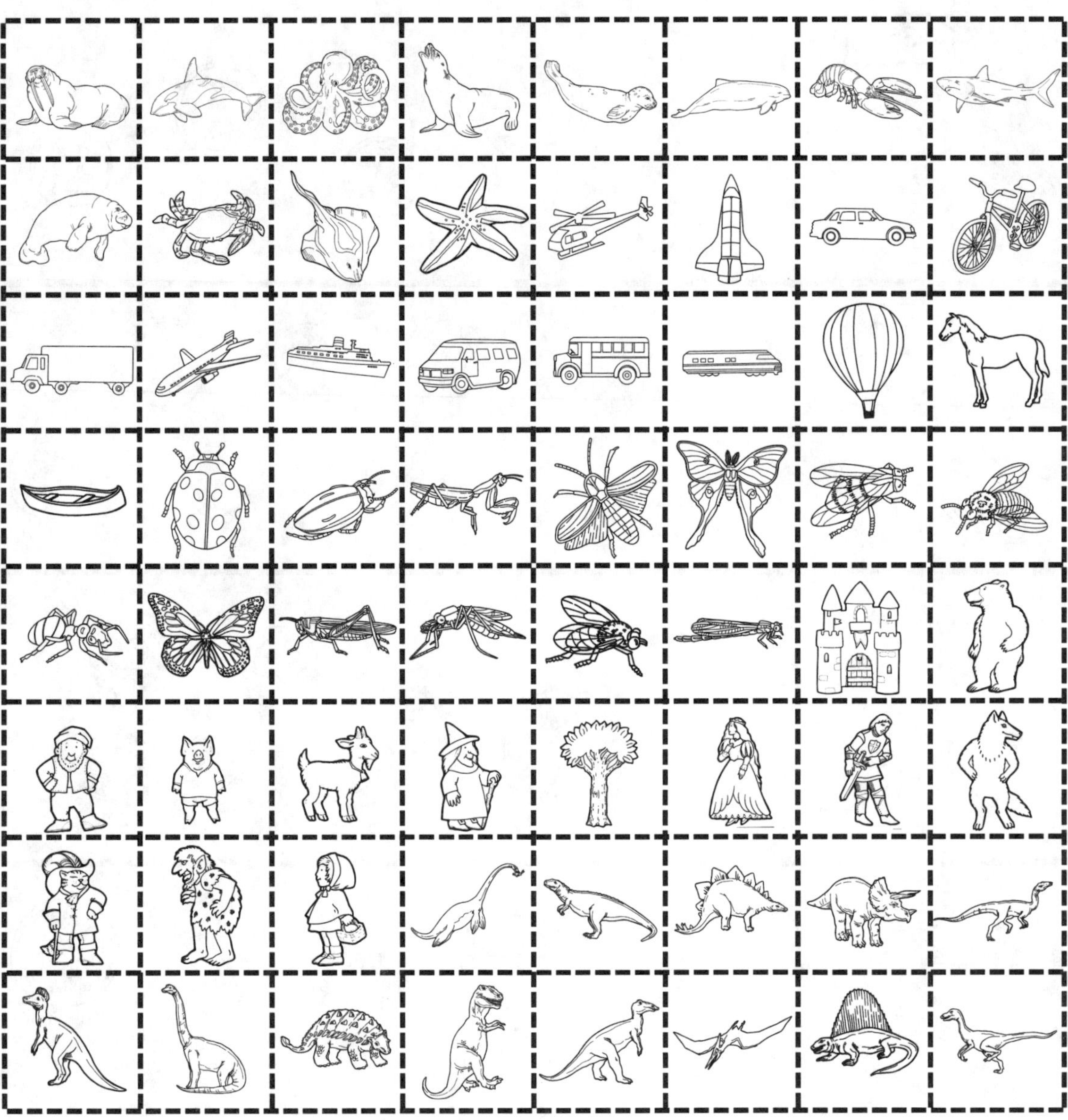

Name: ______________________________

Addition

Write the number sentence for each.

1.

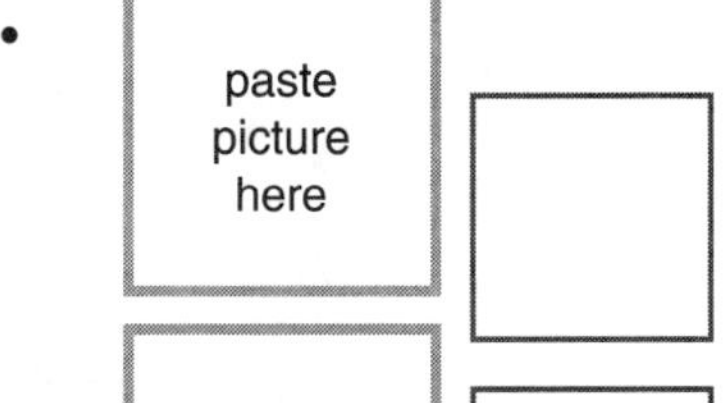

paste picture here

\+ paste picture here

2.

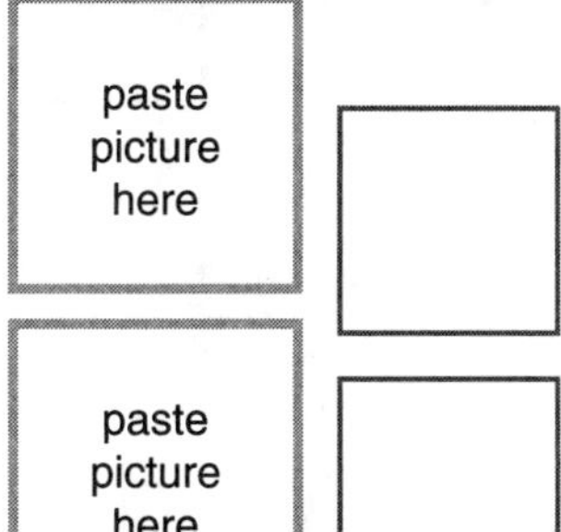

paste picture here

\+ paste picture here

3.

paste picture here

\+ paste picture here

4.

paste picture here

\+ paste picture here

5.

paste picture here

\+ paste picture here

6.

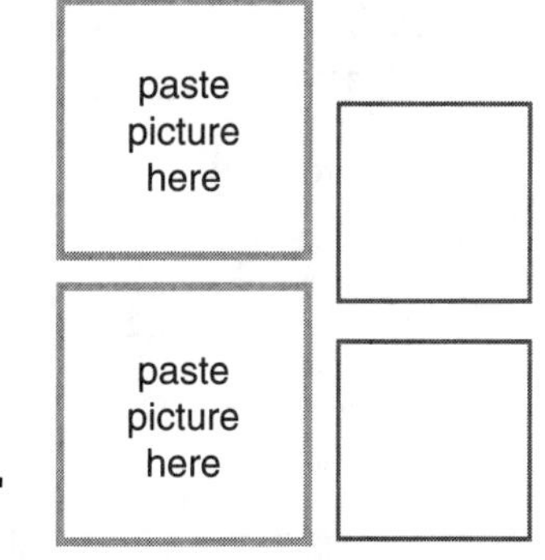

paste picture here

\+ paste picture here

7.

paste picture here

\+ paste picture here

8.

paste picture here

\+ paste picture here

9.

paste picture here

\+ paste picture here

Name: ____________________

Subtraction

1.
paste picture here
– paste picture here

2.
paste picture here
– paste picture here

3.
paste picture here
– paste picture here

4.
paste picture here
– paste picture here

5.
paste picture here
– paste picture here

6.
paste picture here
– paste picture here

7.
paste picture here
– paste picture here

8.
paste picture here
– paste picture here

9.
paste picture here
– paste picture here

Name: ______________________________

Money

Circle the money you would pay for each __________.

1.

add price above

paste picture here

2.

add price above

paste picture here

3.

add price above

paste picture here

4.

add price above

paste picture here

5.

add price above

paste picture here

Name: ______________________________

Estimating and Counting

Top Border	Estimate	Actual
paste picture here		
paste picture here		
paste picture here		
Bottom Border	**Estimate**	**Actual**
paste picture here		
paste picture here		
paste picture here		

Name: ______________________________

Estimating and Counting

Right Border	Estimate	Actual
paste picture here		
paste picture here		
paste picture here		
Left Border	**Estimate**	**Actual**
paste picture here		
paste picture here		
paste picture here		

Notes